The NEW LIFE BLUEPRINT

The NEW LIFE BLUEPRINT

A 21ST CENTURY GUIDE FOR SUCCESS, HEALTH, WEALTH,
AND HAPPINESS IN A COMPLEX WORLD

NATALIA PEART, PH.D.
With CHRISTOPHER BURGE

Forbes | Books

Copyright © 2025 by Natalia Peart, PhD.

All rights reserved. No part of this book may be used or reproduced in any manner whatsoever without prior written consent of the author, except as provided by the United States of America copyright law.

Published by Forbes Books, Charleston, South Carolina.
An imprint of Advantage Media Group.

Forbes Books is a registered trademark, and the Forbes Books colophon is a trademark of Forbes Media, LLC.

Printed in the United States of America.

10 9 8 7 6 5 4 3 2 1

ISBN: 979-8-88750-623-4 (Hardcover)
ISBN: 979-8-88750-624-1 (eBook)

Library of Congress Control Number: 2024918270

Cover design by Megan Elger.
Layout design by Matthew Morse.

This custom publication is intended to provide accurate information and the opinions of the author in regard to the subject matter covered. It is sold with the understanding that the publisher, Forbes Books, is not engaged in rendering legal, financial, or professional services of any kind. If legal advice or other expert assistance is required, the reader is advised to seek the services of a competent professional.

> Since 1917, Forbes has remained steadfast in its mission to serve as the defining voice of entrepreneurial capitalism. Forbes Books, launched in 2016 through a partnership with Advantage Media, furthers that aim by helping business and thought leaders bring their stories, passion, and knowledge to the forefront in custom books. Opinions expressed by Forbes Books authors are their own. To be considered for publication, please visit **books.Forbes.com**.

To our parents:
Albert and Audria Peart
and the memory of Fred and Thelma Burge

CONTENTS

PART 1
PIVOTAL MOMENTS

CHAPTER 1 3
Hear Their Voices

THE SHIFTS

CHAPTER 2 15
Historical Shifts

CHAPTER 3 41
Contextual Shifts

CHAPTER 4 57
Disruptive Shifts

CHAPTER 5 67
Paradigm Shifts

PART 2
MEETING THE MOMENT
THE INNOVATOR BLUEPRINT

CHAPTER 6 79
Overview and Guide

CHAPTER 7 89
Blueprint 1: From Material Plenty
to Health, Wealth, and Happiness

CHAPTER 8 109
Blueprint 2: From Career Ladders
to Playing on Your Court

CHAPTER 9 135
Blueprint 3: From Lifespan to Healthspan

CHAPTER 10 169
Blueprint 4: From Consumer Mindset
to Business of You Mindset

CHAPTER 11 189
Blueprint 5: From 20th Century Education
to 21st Century Preparation

PART 3
DEFINING MOMENTS

CHAPTER 12 213
   The Future Is Human

WHERE TO FROM HERE? 221

ACKNOWLEDGMENTS 225

ABOUT THE AUTHORS 229

REFERENCES 233

INDEX 243

PART 1

PIVOTAL MOMENTS

CHAPTER 1

HEAR THEIR VOICES

Melissa, a twenty-four-year-old college graduate with a degree in journalism, has spent most of her time out of college piecing together a string of freelance jobs just so she can be sure to cover her rent, food, and transportation costs. Her biggest problem hasn't been getting a job. It's been securing a good job that allows her to launch her career and comfortably cover her expenses. Her parents help her out from time to time, and she's now considering whether she should move back home temporarily. "I'm disappointed, because growing up I was told that if I get an education, if I go to college, then I'll be successful," she says. "In reality, it hasn't helped me that much."

Lisa, thirty-nine, and her husband, Jay, forty-three, both work in healthcare. They've been able to not only meet their expenses and take regular vacations but also put away some money—although not as much as they would like—over the years for the education of their two kids. Over the last several years, they've both struggled with having their hours reduced, and Lisa also had to change jobs. For the first time in their lives, they've begun to worry about whether they will still be able to maintain the life they've built. They often talk about feeling that, overnight, they went from having their feet solidly in the middle class to now the fear that they are just a few paychecks away from climbing down and out of where they've worked so hard to be. "We did everything right, but we still are not living our American Dream," Lisa says.

John, fifty-two, worked as a financial analyst his entire career. He made a comfortable income that allowed him and his wife, who has a part-time job with a big retailer, to afford a solid, comfortable life for themselves and their two sons, who are fourteen and sixteen. Following a round of layoffs, John's position was eliminated. After eight months of looking for full-time work, he is still not financially back on his feet, but he does take part-time temporary assignments whenever he can find them. His family members all pitch in, and they count themselves among the fortunate that despite the setbacks, they've still been able to maintain their home. But John worries each day about his chances of recovering the life he had. "It's hard to feel positive when you don't know what's around the corner," he says.

When Richard was fifty, he started planning what he would do in retirement once he stepped away from his job as a manager at a retail company. Now that he is fifty-nine, the reality has finally hit home for him that he is nowhere near retirement. For the last several years, he's been helping his kids pay down their student loan debt. The debt, coupled with the rising costs of living, has left nothing extra for him to put toward his later years. Richard now says, "I no longer see retirement coming anytime soon."

EXTRAORDINARY TIMES CREATE THE URGENCY OF NOW

We are living in one of the most pivotal times in our history—a time that will define us for decades to come. These times are unprecedented, and the world is an exceedingly complex place. The last several years have brought about more change than we have seen in our lifetime, and we are struggling to keep pace in every area of our lives.

The context of our lives has profoundly shifted. Crisis isn't merely the lead headline in the news anymore. It is the backdrop and the filter for our existence. Every time we as individuals think we have caught up and learned how to survive in this climate, change arrives to rewrite the rules once more. It isn't simply the fact that we are experiencing dramatic change that makes us so unsettled; it is the incredible and increasing rate of change that leaves us feeling like we've tumbled into a state of constant imbalance. This change is an order of magnitude greater than anything we have experienced.

THE HEADLINES

These changes also mean that we're experiencing never-before-seen shifts in the way we work and live, as the path to success has fundamentally changed.

We now live with pervasive economic worries, from the high cost of living to inflation worries and the threat of layoffs. Cost-of-living pressures make it harder than ever to reach financial independence. Higher costs, with greater all-around volatility, mean that the ability to support ourselves financially has taken center stage.

The pandemic broke the barriers of how we live and work. While we welcomed the more flexible work arrangements, the pandemic was also a catalyst for a fundamental reexamination and redefining of the role of work in our lives. From quiet quitting to quiet firing to quiet hiring, all the quiet has spoken loudly, and it says that work is broken.

The pandemic also disrupted key life milestones, such as how we go to school and attend social events. Our lifestyles went from seeking work-life balance to coping with a complete work-life blur. And now, even in a more technologically connected world, we are feeling more disconnected than ever. We experienced cascading and collective trauma with no time to heal.

Uncertainty and the faster pace of unexpected change and disruption are the new context and backdrop for our lives. We no longer deal with just a few life changes and transitions in our lifetime. We are dealing with many big shifts and disruptions happening one right after the other or all at once. The rapid pace of change is taking a toll on our psyche. The epidemics of stress and burnout, as well as rising anxiety and other mental health struggles, speak to the constant mental and emotional challenges we face. We live in a world that feels too fragmented, too disjointed, and too noisy.

> This moment is the perfect storm of historic long-term, economically disruptive, and structural changes that have impacted us in all areas of our lives. The shifts have been disruptive and have impacted our financial life, our mental health, the way we work, and our overall lifestyle.

A more complex context and set of problems results in people that feel like even though they are working harder and harder, they are moving in the wrong direction. Instead, they are more insecure and worried. So not only does the world feel out of balance; many are now unsure of how to grow their incomes or their well-being.

THE OLD DREAM AND BLUEPRINT

The old life blueprint we were all taught from a young age was that if you work hard in school, get good grades, and get a degree, you will get a good job that will provide you with safety and security throughout your career. Now, many people are saying they did what they were told to do according to this old blueprint. But many are finding that by doing "everything right" according to the old rules of the past, they are still not arriving at success or their American Dream. Worse yet, some feel as though they are just building a tall house of cards that just leaves them more vulnerable the higher it grows.

NEW CONTEXT

The old life blueprint was more than just a blueprint. It was an implied instruction manual for how we were supposed to live.

The blueprint and rules we have followed all our lives were based on the 20th century's more stable, predictable industrial economy and context, not the more complex digital, globalized, and fast-changing context in which we currently live. The context that gave rise to this old American Dream and blueprint is gone. This is now a more complex world with constant change and disruption as the norm, so the signposts and advice that guided our educational, career, and life choices in the past are obsolete.

THE GAPS

These shifts have left a huge gap between where we are today and how we must adapt. The turbulence, the widening gaps, and the pain all challenge us to bring forth new solutions to bridge the gulf between where we are today and where we need to be, helping us all cross the divide to live more successful, sustainable, and meaningful lives.

We therefore need to shift our paradigm based on the assumptions of this new normal to help us navigate and succeed sustainably in our more complex world. We also need to build a new blueprint to help us navigate this more challenging environment—one that is designed to help us grow through uncertainty without waiting for certainty.

THE OCCASION FOR THIS BOOK

The occasion for our research and this book is based on one critical question: In times of change, uncertainty, and constant disruption, what are the key drivers of success and sustainability? In other words, what are the new blueprints, strategies, and road maps that people, organizations, and the upcoming generation must know to prepare for and successfully navigate this new world?

> We have pioneered a new category of frames and solutions to bridge the gap of how we all now must prepare, navigate, lead, manage, and constantly innovate to sustain our success in this context of change and disruption. The pages of *The New Life Blueprint* represent a journey into what it now takes to achieve success, health, wealth, and happiness in our increasingly complex world.

In part 1, we examine the Pivotal Moments. We ask how and why we got here by examining the historical, contextual, and disruptive shifts along with the broken assumptions that have disrupted the old paths to success. It concludes with the paradigm shift that defines a new view of success and lights the way forward.

In part 2, in order to meet this moment, we have reimagined the old 20th century blueprint and have created a new 21st century blueprint that presents the five critical paradigm shifts that we all must know to shift from obsolete rules and assumptions based on a previous era to the knowledge we need to be successful today and in the future.

We also provide a stage-based road map for navigating uncertainty, building resilience, and redefining success more holistically. Based on our research and multidisciplinary science, we present the five key paradigm shifts that are at the heart of the new Innovator Blueprint.

- **THE WORLD HAS CHANGED**

  We need to have a new relationship with the world around us. The Sustainability shift provides us with new ways to manage our lives and new rules for improving our well-being, standard of living, and quality of life for lifelong sustainability.

- **THE WORLD OF WORK HAS CHANGED**

  We need to have a new relationship with the world of work. The shift from Climbing the Ladder to Playing on Your Court provides us with new ways to manage our work that center our goals and outcomes.

- **WHAT WE WANT FROM THE WORLD HAS CHANGED**

  We need to redefine success in ways that match our more holistic view of our dreams. The Success Redefined shift presents a new life strategy that allows us to prioritize our health and happiness along with our success.

- **HOW WE MUST SEE OURSELVES HAS CHANGED**

    We need to have a new relationship with ourselves. The Business of You mindset shift helps us manage, grow, and innovate in the face of constant change.

- **HOW WE MUST PREPARE FOR THE WORLD HAS CHANGED**

    We need a new view of what it means to be prepared for our new world. The Preparation shift provides us with new ways to prepare for how we must work, live, and navigate our new world throughout our lifetimes.

Part 3 brings us full circle from Pivotal Moments to Defining Moments. There might be a temptation to see the Pivotal Moments we examined in part 1 as simply a story about the challenges we face. But in life, Pivotal Moments are also Defining Moments. They are Defining Moments because challenges also offer opportunities for us not just to meet the world where it is and be affected by it but also to ask how we can affect the world by creating higher ground for all of us. We close with a call to action, a way we all can positively impact our collective human success and fading American Dream.

The journey of *The New Life Blueprint* is collectively a new way forward. It is a new blueprint and life road map for how to prepare and equip ourselves, live our lives, and get to the success, health, wealth, and happiness we seek.

The journey of *The New Life Blueprint* is collectively a new way forward. It is a new blueprint and life road map for how to prepare and equip ourselves, live our lives, and get to the success, health, wealth, and happiness we seek. The journey is also a blueprint for how we can all, as changemakers, answer this moment in a way that allows us not just to see the challenges but also to find the opportunities to reimagine, redefine, and reinvent our American Dream and to create a new, more sustainable future forward.

THE SHIFTS

2

CHAPTER 2

HISTORICAL SHIFTS

Beneath the surface of the big shifts happening in our lives were other seismic shifts in the rules and assumptions of working and living. The rules are so embedded in our psyche that we take for granted this life blueprint and its rules. These rules are the invisible hand that guides our lives.

The old Mastery Blueprint we were all taught from a young age was that if you work hard in school, get good grades, and earn a college degree, you will get a good job that will provide you with safety and security throughout your career. First, you were supposed to find success, then happiness, and then the fulfillment you hoped for based on your hard work. Finally, you were supposed to retire with enough to live on for the rest of your life. Now, most people are saying they did what they were told to do according to this old blueprint, but instead of living their American Dream, they are failing to arrive at success.

THE STATE OF THE DREAM

How exactly did we get here? By *here,* we mean the place where, after a steady climb upward, many are now worried about slipping down the economic ladder and out of the middle class for the first time in their lives. The place where even those who once felt they achieved the dream are experiencing a sense of economic fragility. The place where a lack of belief in the dream is at a record high. The place where children are no longer likely to do better than their parents and the place where we are now starting to wonder if Generation Z is destined to become the economically lost generation.

For millions of people who worked hard and played by the rules, the American Dream seems increasingly out of reach. They are even starting to question the dream itself. Was it just a myth all along? And if it did exist, is the dream just about survival now? Have we reached the end of the so-called American Dream in our lifetime?

There's no doubt that the simultaneous hit of inflation, higher food costs, higher interest rates, a housing crisis, unemployment, and underemployment following the recession brought many households to their knees. Does this perfect storm, though, fully explain the crisis in American life and the questioning of the dream itself that we're still experiencing today? Or does the crisis we're still experiencing have its roots elsewhere, and is it signaling an even deeper shift than we realize? To fully understand the answer to these questions, we need first to understand what the American Dream *really* is.

If you ask people what the American Dream is, the answer will likely include aspirations of having a house, a car or two, a regular vacation, and enough savings to retire and contribute to their children's college education. What's gone largely unnoticed is that this is not how the dream began.

James Truslow Adams first popularized the concept of the American Dream in his 1931 book *Epic of America*: "It is not a dream of motor cars and high wages merely, but a dream of social order in which each man and each woman shall be able to attain the fullest stature of which they are innately capable, and be recognized by others for what they are, regardless of the fortuitous circumstances of birth or position."

He also stated, "The American Dream that has lured tens of millions of all nations to our shores in the past century has not been a dream of merely material plenty, though that has doubtlessly counted heavily ... It has been a dream of being able to grow to fullest development as man and woman, unhampered by the barriers which had slowly been erected in the older civilizations ... which had developed for the benefit of classes rather than for the simple human being of any and every class."

So, the American Dream, as expressed by Adams, was at its core about the *opportunity* to pursue a better life built from ambition and hard work. It was this prospect of a better opportunity that grounded us all in the hope that where we started in life did not need to be where we finished. We could look within ourselves and create a new tomorrow, since the opportunities were endless.

Another defining feature of the American Dream was the belief that children would have the opportunity to have a higher standard of living than their parents. The dream, then, was really about two things: greater opportunity and social mobility. Together, they drove the sacrifice and risk taking. Opportunity and mobility were the reasons behind the pursuit of the American Dream.

Now fast-forward to the economic boom that followed World War II. In this golden time of growth for our nation, our middle class and its share of wealth expanded. We had high employment, and industries were growing. We saw a surge in the housing and automobile industries while new industries like electronics were starting to appear, and businesses were combining to form larger corporations.

During this time of prosperity, many incomes were doubled in a single generation. Millions of families were now part of a growing middle class, which allowed them to sustain a standard of living that was previously only for the wealthy.

For the first time, Americans were able to own automobiles and homes in large numbers. A housing boom, financed by easily affordable mortgages for returning members of the military, was also part of the expansion. Homeownership was now being seen and promoted as a crucial part of having a stake in our society—a part of the American Dream. People were also now moving out of the city and into the suburbs.

At the center of middle-class culture during this period was a growing demand for consumer goods. There was a steady and increasing demand for better cars, clothing, appliances, furniture, and family vacations. Consumerism became a key component of Western society as Americans enjoyed higher disposable income levels than any other country. People were now purchasing goods in an endless attempt to keep up with their neighbors. Through heavy advertising of what was perceived as "the good life" along with loans and credit from banks, Americans were now immediately able to have what they wanted. All in all, this postwar time period was generally one of stability, comfort, and prosperity for Americans.

The qualities that our nation had prided itself on in previous generations, self-reliance and pursuing one's own goals and aspirations, had up until this point been the way we thought of the American Dream.

But by the 1950s, there was a new face of the dream—the corporate man, given that at the time the vast majority of corporate workers were men. William Whyte, an editor for *Fortune* magazine, captured in his landmark book *The Organization Man* the ethos of these executives, who now came to represent the spirit of the American economy and the spirit of the times. The typical organization man was someone who looked forward to staying with their employer for their entire career. The benefits and generous pensions were a huge attraction.

THE TRUE GRAND BARGAIN

While the lure of rewards like money and power and a piece of the dream were obvious incentives, less obvious but often even more compelling—the true grand bargain—was the sense of safety and security that attaining the dream satisfied. We agreed to put control of our destiny in someone else's hands, and in return, we had a clear path upward. If you were loyal to your employer, your employer would always take care of you.

In this grand bargain, we were rewarded with titles, money, and power as visible, outward signs that we had achieved—that we had arrived. Our identities were very much intertwined with the roles we filled in our companies.

What went unnoticed was that the dream was not about who you were and your sense of mobility but about what you could buy. We became consumers as a way to mark success. Instead of employers selling us the dream of the ability to control our own fate and destiny, we were sold the dream of what we could buy—what we could consume in exchange for our loyalty.

Happiness was found in the predictability and security of our jobs.

Over time, happiness and what we could consume were supposed to be deferred. We were supposed to buy our happiness after we became successful. If the previous American Dream was fundamentally about the pursuit of greater opportunity and social mobility, the American Dream transformed into the pursuit of stability and prosperity.

THE OLD LIFE BLUEPRINT

The prevailing narrative we all know and understand about success is that success is a ladder that we could hold on to and climb, rung by rung. Your IQ and talents were the raw material, and your education was critical in your life trajectory. A college degree became the ticket you needed to punch for entry into the middle class. Not only was it the ticket in; a solid education helped to level the playing field if you did not come from a family or background that already had lots of networks and connections.

Your education did something else for you: it was a safety net. If one job did not work out but you had a solid educational background, you were confident that you would find another job in your field or that you could transfer your skills to another career. Since the upward climb was supposed to be fairly smooth, job hopping was a career killer. You didn't seem serious about your career if you could not find a job that you could commit to and stay with for a long period of time.

Just as important, the climb upward included knowing how to pay your dues. You were expected to work hard and wait/hope to be noticed by your boss, who had the power to decide the next steps on your climb. It was your boss who ultimately controlled your career, not you. In this way, your identity was intertwined with the roles you served within your company.

The old life blueprint provided a basic level of predictability and life stability. It was an imperfect script but one that we all knew and could easily recite.

Of course, the most important part of the old life, or Mastery Blueprint, was the carrot at the end of the path—the success our hard work was supposed to afford us. While the lure of rewards like money, power, and a piece of the American Dream were obvious incentives, less obvious but often even more compelling to many was the sense of safety and security. Hard work used to be rewarded with economic security.

> You were expected to work hard and wait/hope to be noticed by your boss, who had the power to decide the next steps on your climb. It was your boss who ultimately controlled your career, not you.

Now, the rules have changed, and we are experiencing a broken path to success at all stages. With a globalized economy and the rapid advancement of technology, the long-term employment pact that used to exist between employer and employee—that is, giving lifetime employment for lifetime loyalty—is now a short-term agreement that is constantly up for renewal and renegotiation. We are now in a time when employment is becoming more unstable, and unemployment or underemployment is becoming more common.

Gone are the days of thinking that job security would come after our hard work in school and getting a job with a big company that would take care of us. That was then, and this is now. Everything that we were told was safe no longer is. You should no longer expect to get your ticket into the middle class by obtaining your degree and working your way up the ladder by putting your head down, being a team player, and waiting to be recognized. This old blueprint no longer consistently translates to success the way it did in the past, and now the ladder to success seems rungless.

THE STATE OF EDUCATION

The foundation of the dream was a good education. The degree was the ticket to the American Dream. Your education was supposed to help you gain a solid footing in the world of work and insulate you from slipping through the cracks, since you would always have your education to fall back on. Recently, we have seen a number of challenges to the role education plays in connecting us to the future of work and, therefore, its overall value relative to cost.

NO CLEAR FOOTHOLDS OR LEGS UP

Education is no longer the safe and reliable ticket to success that it once was. The foundation of the American Dream was a good education. It was supposed to guarantee entry into the middle class and help us not fall back. Now, the traditional ticket to success feels broken.

The Mastery Blueprint for Success that we have followed for generations held as its core the ideal of most high school graduates earning a college degree. Since 1965, the federal government has made loans available to any college-bound eighteen-year-old with a high school diploma. Between 1965 and 2011, university enrollment increased nearly fourfold to twenty-one million as the earning differential between high school and college graduates expanded.

SKILL-NEED MISALIGNMENT

The digital revolution was such a powerful historical force that by the end of the 20th century, nearly every country was connected and many businesses already had websites. By the start of the 21st century, cell phones had become a common possession. These shifts demanded that formal education be more nimble so that students could learn a quickly emerging set of skills to meet changing labor market demands. Yet campuses were slow to adapt, if they did at all. The result of the combination of more college graduates and weaker learning outcomes has diluted the signal provided by a degree from less prestigious colleges.

ESCALATING COSTS AND STUDENT LOAN DEBT CRISIS

The average cost of an undergraduate degree increased by 169 percent between 1980 and 2020. After adjusting for inflation, college tuition has increased 747.8 percent since 1963. These staggering increases mean each new generation has a heftier financial burden when they graduate.

Given the escalating costs of education, it is not surprising that student debt has more than doubled over the last two decades. As of March 2023, about forty-four million US borrowers collectively owed more than $1.6 trillion in federal student loans. Additional private loans bring that total to above $1.7 trillion, surpassing auto loans and credit card debt.

SHIFTING MARKET

Many students choose their field of study not only based on personal interest; they also take into account—or in some cases they base their decisions mostly on—potential job prospects and how lucrative and stable the industry is based on past history. In the past, becoming a doctor or a lawyer, for example, was seen as a safe, prestigious, and highly upwardly mobile career.

More recently, working in the tech field had seemed like one of the most stable careers one could have. But now, after a period of widespread cuts, that is no longer the case.

Newly minted management consultants are also finding that after years of a business pandemic-related boom, the industry is on shakier ground. For many, years of educational investment might not pay off in the way they had hoped.

Given that higher education funnels students into prescribed majors that they are supposed to connect to their chosen industry, when industries decline, such as in the media industry recently, many students whose training is narrower and more specific have been left searching for how to regain their footing, since industries are not as stable as they once were.

> "I went to college and followed every step I needed to; I majored in computer science in the hope of securing a safe career. I thought my future was secure, but I was wrong. It's been harder than I thought to land a job. I couldn't quite get my head around the fact that I couldn't find a job. After a long search, I am finally using my skills at a retail company, not a tech company as I thought."
> —Ashley

GREATER FOCUS ON SKILLS

Since major employers have begun to drop their long-held degree requirements in favor of a greater emphasis on skills, students are now seeing that recruiters globally are five times more likely to search for new hires by skills than by focusing only on higher education. In fact, nearly half of US companies intend to eliminate bachelor's degree requirements for some job positions next year, though this does not mean that degrees will no longer be considered in the hiring process.

DEGREE AND JOB MISMATCH

Recent studies show that approximately half the students who earn college diplomas find themselves working in jobs that don't require a bachelor's degree, such as retail and hospitality, or utilize the skills they acquired in obtaining one.

If a graduate's first job is in a low-paying field or out of line with their interests, this can have long-lasting career consequences. Many college graduates remain underemployed even ten years after college. That may be because many employers, particularly in competitive fields, requiring college-level skills, also have work experience requirements. This requirement favors hiring candidates who have spent years in the workforce obtaining the needed skills versus those who only earned a degree in that field.

Another study found that a decade after enrolling in college, one in four graduates earned less than $32,000, which is the median annual income for high school graduates.

IS A DEGREE STILL WORTH IT? IT'S COMPLICATED...

Choice of major matters. While getting a college degree is traditionally viewed as the ticket to the American Dream, it is not necessarily a ticket to a higher-paying job. One of the most important determinants of postgraduation employment prospects is a college student's major—in some cases, it can be even more important than the type of institution a student attends.

For example, while focusing on science, technology, engineering, and mathematics (STEM) subjects is not a guarantee of college-level employment and high wages, a study found that focusing on more career-oriented majors, like health services such as nursing, might give graduates a better shot at getting compensated for the skills they acquire.

Internships matter. There are also other ways to boost the prospects of a fruitful and meaningful career that make a college degree a worthy investment. Internships and relevant experience help. For example, securing an internship while pursuing one's undergraduate degree can reduce the risk of underemployment by almost 50 percent.

> "As a business major, I was able to secure a job as a research analyst when I graduated. Looking back, I would say that building my network early helped me open doors for myself. The people I met at industry events as a student and alumni who mentored me changed my life. They helped me secure a summer internship and get my foot in the door for job offers after I graduated."
> —Robert

While it is still true that getting a college education can still be worth the investment in the long run, depending on what major you choose and what you expect to do with it after you graduate, these findings add fuel to the debate over the value of a college education, as its cost has soared while the return on the investment has become inconsistent. Many, such as Matt Sigelman, president of Burning Glass Institute, which conducts research on the future of work and of workers, believe that "it's not that a degree isn't worth it"; the problem is that "it's worth it to too few people."

Losing confidence. These sobering findings come as more Americans question the eroding value of a college degree and as more employers are dropping higher-education degree requirements altogether.

Not only has undergraduate enrollment declined since 2011, translating into three million fewer students on campus, but polls indicate that in the past decade, the percentage of Americans who expressed a lot of confidence in higher education fell from 57 percent to 36 percent. Two-thirds of high school students believe they do not need a college degree, and nearly half of parents say they would prefer not to send their children to a four-year college after high school, even if there were no obstacles, financial or otherwise.

> "You're told your entire life: 'Go to college, get a bachelor's degree, and your life will be set after that.' It's been a year since I graduated. I am still looking for a full-time job while I learn to adapt to my reality and figure it out one day at a time. It will just take some patience in this labor market."
> —Taylor

THE STATE OF WORK

If a good education was seen as the foundation of the American Dream, then obtaining a secure job with health and retirement benefits that also allowed you to climb the ladder of success was at the heart of the dream.

Since the end of World War II, the American Dream has been largely defined as the ability to attain stable employment with comfortable compensation and benefits. For many, such middle-class promises often meant spending their entire occupational careers with a single company, which afforded enterprise organizations both loyalty and stability from their employees in return for similar loyalty and commitment.

RETHINKING RISK AND THE TRUE GRAND BARGAIN

As discussed, we used to think that once we found our lane and a good job in that lane, the job would last us a lifetime, and we would have a sense of security. We would never have to worry again. In fact, employers encouraged us to think of our bosses and coworkers as our family. As long as we paid our dues and gave our skills and talents to our company, we would be rewarded in exchange with the trappings of success, such as promotions and prestige in the short run and job stability and security in the long run.

Even with this broken contract, there was another problem with this grand bargain we made with employers. The fine print said that success would come by working hard and waiting for someone else, usually your boss, to notice you and help you move your career forward. But you needed to wait for someone else to tell you which of your skills were most valuable, wait for the next promotion, and wait to get someone else's permission to explore other avenues if that was what you wanted to do.

In this grand bargain, your value was based on what someone else decided. The irony was that the higher we climbed up the company ladder, the more at risk we felt because it was now no longer just our job on the line. It was our family health insurance, our home mortgage, our car payments, the kids' college tuition, and so on. In exchange for this thing called "security," we handed the keys to our lives to someone else.

THE GREAT RISK SHIFT: FROM DEFINED BENEFIT TO DEFINED CONTRIBUTION

The 1970s brought America one of the most dramatic changes facing workers—the transformation from defined-benefit to defined-contribution retirement plans. Employees would be able to contribute their own money in a tax-advantaged way to an account to supplement any other retirement benefits they had with tax incentives for the employer also to contribute. The number of years a worker spends with an employer is no longer an investment in the employee's retirement. As a result, the typical US employee's responsibility for developing a sustainable retirement income has shifted from the employer to the individual.

Today, according to a recent study, retirement planning for millennials and Gen Zers looks much different than it did for older generations. Pensions and Social Security were once the norm. Today, they're the exception. Social Security will likely make up a smaller percentage of retirement funding for younger Americans.

THE STATE OF THE SOCIAL CONTRACT

White- and blue-collar workers frequently had an unwritten contract with their employers. It was an understood "social contract" that offered both parties security. The commonly understood social contract

THE NEW LIFE BLUEPRINT

between employer and employee was characterized by lifelong security of employment and career advancement as long as the employee performed. In this way of being, the weight of responsibility rested with the employer.

> White- and blue-collar workers frequently had an unwritten contract with their employers. It was an understood "social contract" that offered both parties security. The commonly understood social contract between employer and employee was characterized by lifelong security of employment and career advancement as long as the employee performed.

By the close of the 20th century, the expectation of one job for life had fallen. Since the 1990s, businesses have outsourced labor to contract and gig workers. This means that instead of long-term stability, employment relationships are now more transitory. Workers also do not have stability and benefits, no matter how hard they work.

For some gig workers, rather than providing them with flexibility and freedom, gig work resulted in perpetual work with not enough hours. At least 17 percent of the workforce is assigned to unstable work schedules. These people tend to be lower income and work in retail, hospitality and leisure, professional and business settings, and health services.

The problem is that when people don't know what their work shift is going to be from week to week, they can't plan for free time, childcare, time with their family, or anything that furthers their long-term career prospects, such as taking courses. As a result, people have experienced hard work but on very unrewarding terms.

THE BROKEN SOCIAL CONTRACT

We've also said goodbye to the social contract; the unwritten rules that governed our expectations are gone. Previously, there was an exchange of the promise of benefits, security, and a defined pension for hard work and loyalty. None of that exists today. A recent WSJ poll showed that Americans value "hard work" less than they used to.

Sixty-seven percent of those surveyed said hard work is "very important" to them. That was a sixteen-percentage-point decrease from when they first asked that question in 1998, when 83 percent said hard work was very important. For many, the problem is "the payoffs of hard work have been insecurity." People are now choosing to have more of an attitude of work to live as opposed to live to work.

THE LURE OF STABILITY AND SECURITY IS GONE

In years past, hard work could be accompanied by the security of a salary, along with a defined benefit pension, retiree medical care, etc. None of that exists today. However, many people took on student debt and mortgages and built lives based on this promise of stability. There was a built-in assumption that if you put the work in on the front end, the rewards on the back end would be greater. This promise has now dissipated. People increasingly feel that they are being told to "make sacrifices above and beyond to make the company prosperous—prosperity that [they] are very unlikely to share in." Workers realize that this "hypertransactional relationship between employers and employees where no one owes anyone anything" is not what they want. Still, it is the one they must now adjust to.

> George, a married father of two, moved his family from Denver to Austin to take a job at an online education technology company. After nine months, he was laid off and has since struggled to find a new job. He said he saw his job reposted for lower pay shortly after he was laid off. George, forty-five, has depleted close to $300,000 in retirement and emergency savings to relocate and pay for two children's college costs. His and his wife's part-time jobs are keeping the family afloat.

THE RISE OF WORK TRENDS

On social media, trends from quiet quitting to quiet firing to quiet hiring spoke loudly. Collectively, the proliferation of trends signaled something much more important than the specifics of the trends themselves. The relationship between employers and employees feels broken, and people are left filling in the gap of the new rules in the absence of a clear set of rules and a social contract. Even getting laid off or fired, once a private process, is now being shared. Now, layoffs have become more normalized and understandable for these possible reasons:

- Perhaps it's a way for those who have been laid off to feel as though they are gaining some power and control back in a powerless situation.
- Perhaps it's a way for those who have been laid off to show strength in numbers even when they feel vulnerable.
- Perhaps it's a way, in a time of mass-email faceless layoffs, to simply say, "I matter."

THE SOCIAL CONTRACT PROVIDED MORE THAN WE UNDERSTOOD

The old blueprint of clearly defined career paths and ladder rungs to climb helped us know how to gain momentum in our careers, as they were the rules for success in our chosen fields. The implied social contract was more than just a contract. The security of stable employment provided enough stability in the present so one could work toward purchasing a home, cars, and other basics for living and creating our desired lives in the present. The health and retirement benefits we received ensured that our futures were taken care of. Therefore, these more stable career paths and the social contract we operated under provided the infrastructure and scaffolding for our lives. So, we valued not only the salary from the careers themselves; we also needed the benefits to provide the infrastructure to lead and manage our lives securely.

THE STATE OF CAREER PATHS

Another defining feature of the old blueprint was that, after your college degree, you had a clear foothold and leg up to the work world, and you were supposed to have access to clear career paths and ladders for upward career momentum. Across the recent past, we've learned that linear career paths are a thing of the past; they no longer exist. The CEO of LinkedIn, a professional networking site, says that for the past fifteen years, one of the most requested features on LinkedIn has been a tool that shows members what a typical career path looks like for a given role. "It turns out the data tells us nothing, because there truly is no linear career path," he says. "I think it's helped a lot of people understand that, first and foremost, you have to put your career in your own hands."

THE PATH IS BROKEN

The dream was not just a dream in isolation. It also had an embedded system in which the structure and currency moved us forward if we did our part. The underlying system that undergirded the dream and helped propel us forward is gone. It provided the structure, the currency, and the momentum to propel us forward. This is in part why this dream is fading—there is no real underlying infrastructure connecting our steps from education to work or propelling us forward once we are working.

WHEN THE SOLUTION BECOMES THE PROBLEM

When we realized the path to success in the old blueprint was no longer working, we attempted to fix it by adopting hustle-and-grind or boss culture. These solutions suggested that if we simply doubled down, worked harder, and did more, we would eventually get to success.

Of course, hard work is a good thing. Still, these solutions did not acknowledge that the context and assumptions behind our old blueprint for success had shifted, and emptying ourselves to succeed without the life infrastructure that accompanied the grind would not fully solve the problems. These solutions failed to acknowledge that the problem was not hard work. The problem was that, unlike the previous generations, where the payoff for hard work was greater security, the payoff for hard work was now insecurity. Researchers have said the problem isn't that Americans don't want to work hard. Particularly with the rise of the gig economy, workers have lost stability, income, benefits, and social status no matter how hard they've worked. The problem is that "the payoffs of hard work have been insecurity."

> "No matter how hard we hustle, the statistics say that most of us will still hit that proverbial glass ceiling. 'I do think that there's a very seductive element to [the idea that] if I work hard enough, if I do the right networking, if I have the right internet presence, then I will get the life that I want,' says Samhita Mukhopadhyay, former executive editor of *Teen Vogue* ... And that has certainly worked for a handful of women. But for most of us, in the absence of universal health care, worker protections, and affordable childcare, those illusions have crumbled."
> —Ann Friedman, *Elle* magazine

STATE OF THE OLD BLUEPRINT

Education, work, and the infrastructure of how we create and manage our lives are not the only things that are broken. The old blueprint and the assumptions that came with it are also broken.

The purpose of the life blueprint was to provide a basic level of predictability and life stability based on a script that was not perfect but broadly held to be true. We now know that not only is the old dream in question; many of the assumptions and rites of passage that came from our blueprint are also broken.

BROKEN ASSUMPTIONS

The effects of all the broken steps on the path to success extend beyond what we can see. This is also a story about broken assumptions and rites of passage. We had markers that helped us define our life stages and gauge whether our lives were on track, such as obtaining a good education in the first twenty years of life, maximizing our earnings, building our lives for the next thirty-plus years, and then comfortably retiring after that hard work. These markers now feel broken. Not only do many feel as though they are no longer moving upward, but for all the hard work, many now find themselves in survival mode and feeling like they are falling through the cracks.

> Your twenties used to be the time when you committed to marriage or raising young children. Now, those responsibilities don't come for most people until almost a decade later.

Your twenties used to be the time when you committed to marriage or raising young children. Now, those responsibilities don't come for most people until almost a decade later. As one person put it, "Many people who do all the right things—invest in education and work hard—are still struggling to make ends meet."

SHRINKING FAITH IN THE DREAM

Many are finding that by doing "everything right" according to the old rules of the past, they are not moving toward their American Dream. They are just building a tall house of cards that is vulnerable to coming apart as soon as there is one unexpected event, since we no longer have sturdy scaffolding and infrastructure to undergird our lives.

We no longer have the same system to guide us (i.e., education that leads to clear career paths). We do not have support for our movement forward (i.e., upward trajectory of career ladders). We no longer have greater security and the rewards that we need (i.e., all the benefits that we need to live a bigger life and increase the standard and quality of our lives in exchange for our hard work). We no longer know how to run the race.

At the core of the original American Dream was the opportunity to take your destiny into your own hands. It was a unifying vision that with our hard work, we could live to our fullest and our kids would be better off. Now, we don't seem to be able to do that.

According to recent polls, Americans are increasingly unlikely to believe that those who work hard will get ahead and that their children will be better off than they are.

When asked whether they believe "the American Dream—that if you work hard, you'll get ahead—still holds true," just 36 percent said it does, compared to 18 percent who said it never held true and 45 percent who said it once held true but not anymore.

These results denote a stark difference from surveys in 2012 and 2016, when 53 percent and 48 percent, respectively, said the American Dream held true. While different pollsters took the polls, the downward trend is clear. Compared to the previous polls, the percentage of people who believe that the American Dream was never a reality also more than doubled.

Opportunity Insight's longitudinal research on upward mobility trends showed that in 1940, a child had a 90 percent chance of earning more than their parents. In 1955, it was a 70 percent chance, but by the 1990s, the chance was 50 percent—no better than a coin toss.

In another recent poll, a record-low 19 percent of respondents said they were confident their children's generation would be better off than their own.

The diminishing faith in the American Dream in its current form is not surprising, given the broken education and work paths and the lack of a social contract that provided the infrastructure and upward momentum for the dream.

THE NEW LIFE BLUEPRINT

DEATH OF THE DREAM?

Now, with a broken path all along the way and no social contract, we are left asking questions such as these: What is the reward for loyalty and hard work? What propels us forward in our own dreams for more years? What will provide greater stability that will allow us to build our life of true fulfillment, not just consume our way to happiness?

This dream, it seems, has run its course.

CHAPTER 3

CONTEXTUAL SHIFTS

PRICED OUT OF THE DREAM

Even beyond the historic shifts in education and work on the path to success, many are currently experiencing another problem. They feel priced out of the American Dream, as they feel they can no longer afford it. What has made the idea of the traditional American Dream feel so out of reach? The high cost of education, the rising cost of living, and the increased costs and barriers to homeownership, all in the context of stagnant wages, are some of the factors that are now making the dream feel out of reach.

Over the last few years, people have endured high inflation; high interest rates; and rising prices for basic needs like groceries, child care, and insurance, which have stretched household budgets thin. High mortgage rates and increasing home prices have made it more expensive and challenging to purchase a home. Six-figure salaries that once seemed high enough to guarantee a middle-class lifestyle now feel to many like enough to just get by.

> Amanda and her husband, Roger, earn a combined annual salary of $110,000 and have health insurance benefits. However, the couple says their income covers their monthly expenses, including rent for their two-bedroom apartment, utilities, groceries, and gas, but not much else. A $500 emergency-room visit for one of their young sons drained most of their savings. They're unsure how they'll find room in their budget to cover summer activities for their boys.

A CHANGING ECONOMIC CONTEXT

Millions of Americans got used to a decade-long economic boom that also brought low interest rates that many took for granted. But as we have all recently experienced, our economic context can change swiftly.

The economic booms. According to the National Bureau of Economic Research, the longest period of economic expansion occurred in the United States between June 2009 and February 2020, which marked the beginning of a recession. This economic expansion lasted 128 months, the longest in the history of US business cycles dating back to 1854. The previous record for economic expansion was the 120 months from March 1991 to March 2000. During these economic booms, lower interest rates created a favorable environment for business start-ups and investing.

Inflation. Historically, according to the Minneapolis Federal Reserve, the inflation rate fluctuation in the 1990s was relatively low, ranging from 4.2 percent to 1.6 percent. But the 2020s have seen much higher fluctuations. June 2022 saw a 9.1 percent increase in inflation, and it took a full year to get inflation to 3.0 percent.

Wages. According to the US Department of Labor, the federal minimum wage increased four times during the 1990s. The last increase was in 2009, to $7.25, which is where it currently stands. Wage stagnation has been a major hindrance to financial security and wealth building.

According to an Economic Policy Institute analysis of data from the US Bureau of Labor Statistics, hourly pay increased by 14.8 percent from 1979 to 2022. However, productivity increased by 64.7 percent during the same time period—4.4 times more than pay.

Costs of living. Over the past decade, many families have experienced a rise in the costs of basic living necessities. As the cost of living continues to rise in America, many families are struggling to make ends meet in the short run, which in turn makes it difficult for them to attain economic security in the long run.

Cost of food. Food has become much more expensive over the last few years. Between 2019 and 2023, food prices increased by 25 percent. In comparison, the twenty-year average inflation rate on retail food is 2.5 percent per year, according to the US Department of Agriculture. For the average household, this means that the same basket of groceries that would have cost $100 in 2019 now costs $125.51 in 2024.

Cost of housing. Housing costs have soared and wages haven't kept up, according to data in a new report. Homebuyers need to earn between 50 and 80 percent more than they did prepandemic to comfortably afford a house in this market, Zillow says, and rent has more than doubled since 2000, far outpacing the growth of incomes over the same period, according to Moody's Analytics.

Half of all renters in the United States spend more than 30 percent of their income on rent and utilities, more than at any other time in history, according to a report by Harvard's Joint Center for Housing Studies.

> "It's like we can't breathe." Keith and Heather, both forty-three, earn $140,000 combined from their jobs and side gigs. Yet affordability is a "constant conversation" in their household. "With $140,000, I feel like we should be able to have a little extra," Keith says. "With three kids, we can pay our bills, but there's never anything extra. We don't go out to dinner or travel." They cut cable and canceled subscriptions. While they don't have car payments, they're worried one of their cars will break down and they won't be able to buy another one. They've been forced to use credit cards for everyday purchases.

THE BIG SQUEEZE

This cumulative greater financial demand placed on us now serves as the backdrop of our lives. For many, this weight of daily existence has exacted too heavy a toll in the short run, even beyond our inability to achieve our personal American Dream goals in the long run. Long-term dream chasing has been replaced with short-term financial survival. As the financial pain builds, we are financially vulnerable. As households face multiple hits from higher inflation, interest, and costs of living, credit card use has swelled, and delinquencies are among their highest rates in a decade.

Additionally, auto loan delinquencies are higher than they were at the peak of the Great Recession. Many Americans are now living in financial distress, at least some of the time. While it is unsurprising that people earning less struggle more, financial vulnerability is now happening across the income spectrum. According to a 2024 survey, more than 70 percent of Americans live paycheck to paycheck at least some of the time, while nearly 50 percent of Americans live paycheck to paycheck all the time. This includes 51 percent of Americans who make more than $100,000 a year who say they still run out of money. Forty-four percent of Americans can't pay an unexpected $1,000 expense from savings.

> "I received a $500 bill for a recent X-ray after an unexpected medical scare. I was earning an entry-level salary as a digital marketer at the time, and the shock of having to figure out how to cover this unexpected expense sent my pulse racing and stress through the roof."
> —Anthony

As a consequence of greater distress, many Americans cope by diverting finances, downsizing their standard and quality of life, and delaying their life plans.

WE ARE DIVERTING FINANCES

As the cost of living continues to rise, people have pulled from their savings accounts and put away less each month after recording a record level of savings after the pandemic. The 401(k) is now doubling as a retirement account and a source of emergency funds for more Americans. According to internal data from Vanguard Group, a record share of 401(k) account holders took early withdrawals from their accounts for financial emergencies.

WE HAVE A DOWNSIZED STANDARD AND QUALITY OF LIFE

People are shifting away from name-brand items to store-brand items in grocery stores. They are switching to discount stores or buying fewer items like snacks or gourmet foods. More people are buying used cars. Median new home sizes are at a thirteen-year low, since the price of homes is increasingly out of reach. With our decreased purchasing power, for many it feels like they are paying more and getting less from living and life. Even worse, it feels like we are shrinking inside our lives.

> As a treasure-hunting grocery shopper, Marie drives all over town in pursuit of the best deals. Every Sunday, to keep her household grocery bill under $250 a week, she sits at her kitchen table to plan the meals for her family of four and where she'll purchase each ingredient. She shops more grocery store private-label brands than she did before. She also checks to see what is on sale that week or what she can buy in bulk for savings.

THE SHRINKING MIDDLE CLASS

As a growing number of families are struggling to afford the basics of living, a Bankrate survey finds that Americans are over two times more likely to feel financially insecure than secure. While there is no clear description of what it means to be middle class, the Pew Research Center defines middle income as those with an annual household income that was two-thirds to double the national median income in 2020, or about $52,000 to $156,000 annually in 2020 dollars for a household of three.

Yet for many Americans, the idea of being middle class is more related to the feeling they have rather than the amount of income they earn. A 2022 Gallup survey found that 38 percent of Americans identify as "middle class"—an identification that has been shrinking since the Great Recession. Since then, Americans have been more likely to call themselves working- or lower-class than middle-class members. People who had expectations of being middle class are finding that they can't meet the basic expenses of a middle-class life, paying for food, rent, and childcare all at the same time. Elise Gould, a senior economist at the Economic Policy Institute, says that for many Americans, the term "middle class" means having a certain amount of economic security.

In a recent *Washington Post* survey intended to determine which indicators of financial security and stability were necessary to be middle class, nine out of ten respondents agreed on these six indicators:

1. Having a secure job
2. Ability to save money for the future
3. Ability to afford an emergency $1,000 expense without debt
4. Ability to pay all bills on time without worry
5. Having health insurance
6. Ability to retire comfortably

The hallmark of the American Dream is that most people expect to have a solid, middle-class life—a house, a car, a pension, and retirement—but that expectation is increasingly out of reach. "The ability to afford the basic middle-class standard of living is becoming increasingly elusive, even for some in the upper middle class."

> "When I was younger, I assumed that once I made six figures, I'd be set. I would be able to buy a home and be worry-free. But even with $130,000 a year, I worry about the future. Right now, owning a home is out of the question. It will take me about eight years to save up for the down payment. I feel way behind on attaining what I assumed would be something I should be able to afford with my salary."
> —Michael

WE ARE DELAYING LIFE PLANS

A Wells Fargo Money Study found that three out of five Americans are worried about their financial future amid high prices, rising interest rates, and ongoing uncertainty. As a result, 67 percent of people were cutting back on their expenses while 45 percent reported delaying life plans because navigating life in the present leaves little room to consider significant life decisions down the road.

> "As Gen Xers, Christopher and I often recall that growing up, neither of our families had a lot of money. I am originally from Panama, so when my parents immigrated to the United States, it was to make sure my brother and I could have a better life. They did whatever they could to give us whatever they could. Christopher's father literally did not have indoor plumbing when he was a child, so as an adult, his father worked days while his mother worked nights to make sure their three boys were well provided for. Christopher and I both grew up having a good roof over our heads; our parents always managed to clothe and feed us, and we went out for

> dinner occasionally as kids. Yet for many today, these kinds of markers, like owning a home and being able to provide for your family without constant worry, seem like a far-off wish."
> —Dr. Natalia Peart

THE ECONOMY IS PERSONAL

While a more challenging cost-of-living context has had a broad effect on our lives, the impact of these challenges is personal. The data alone does not tell the full story of the impact of these shifts. Economic pressures have impacted progression at all life stages.

GEN Z: UNABLE TO LAUNCH

Given their current economic context of higher prices, stagnant wages, and expensive student loans, achieving full financial independence has become more difficult than ever. Young adults today are much more likely than their parents to have a four-year college degree, work full time, and have higher wages than their parents did thirty years ago. However, according to a recent report by the Pew Research Center, Gen Zers are also less likely to own a home, be married, or have children. Additionally, about one-third still live with their parents. Other studies also show that most people with student loans say they've had to delay one or more key life milestones because of their debt.

Today's young adults are reaching those key milestones later than their parents did in the early 1990s. As important life milestones—such as moving out, buying a home, and having children—get pushed down the road, Gen Zers can feel that they are falling behind, and

73 percent of Gen Z respondents said today's economy makes them hesitant to set long-term financial goals.

> "Soon after graduating, I realized that one job wasn't cutting it. My pay barely covered what I needed monthly, so I had to get two part-time jobs to cover my basic needs."
> —Cameron

MILLENNIALS: HARD TO BUILD LIFE INFRASTRUCTURE

The thirty-something American Dream used to be something like this: "You're married, you have kids, and you own your starter home." But things have shifted. Millennials are getting married later, if they marry at all. They're having kids later, if at all. And forget the home. Millennials feel priced out of the housing market, and this shapes their view of their economic life. Millennials entered the workforce during the Great Recession. They were saddled with debt, underemployed, and unable to accumulate wealth. Now, as they reach this new life stage of peak home-buying and household-forming age, housing affordability is at forty-year lows, and mortgage rates are near forty-year highs. That's helping establish a new millennial milestone for some: moving out of the family home, not having roommates, and living alone. Living alone has now become a luxury.

> "I'm thirty, and I live in New York. Most of my friends who are older than I am have roommates. Thankfully, I don't have to do that."
> —Alison

GEN X: STRETCHED TOO THIN

As younger generations struggle to navigate a tough housing market, student loans, and challenging economies, many people are depending on their parents longer than expected. As a result, 81 percent of Gen Xers report feeling financial stress at least sometimes.

Generation X will be the first to reach retirement under the 401(k) plans in the United States, a result of the big change that shifted the responsibility to save for retirement from employers to individual employees. While Gen Xers reported that on average they will need roughly $1.1 million in savings to retire comfortably, the median account balance is only $10,000, and 40 percent have zero savings.

> "I'm not just worried about myself—I have young kids, and my parents are getting old. How do I care for everyone and myself?"
> —Katherine

BOOMERS: UNABLE TO RETIRE

According to recent studies, many Americans nearing retirement age have nothing set aside to pay for their lives after they stop working. More than half of Americans over the age of sixty-five are living off less than $30,000 a year, according to 2022 Census data. Meanwhile, 45 percent of middle-income households risk not keeping up with their preretirement living standards once they turn sixty-five, according to data from the Center for Retirement Research. These findings are complicated by the fact that Social Security may not be able to provide the same support for younger workers when they reach retirement age.

> "As the cost of living is quickly outpacing my Social Security benefits, I fear I won't be able to afford my care. After working my whole life, I can't age with dignity."
> —Scott

THE STATE OF FINANCIAL WELL-BEING

An American Psychological Association (APA) study found that 72 percent of Americans feel stressed about money at least some of the time. Recent economic difficulties mean that even more of us are facing financial struggles and hardships.

Financial stress is a feeling of worry and anxiety related to money. It could be day-to-day concerns like not having enough money to cover basic needs or a general sense of being unable to manage debt or achieve personal goals like buying a home or affording a car because of fund shortages.

Whether people are looking to get their life started or to retire comfortably, stress is a rampant part of American life, and much of it is caused by financial insecurity. A lack of economic certainty and resilience is affecting our well-being. This stress has forced a lot of Americans to focus more on short-term goals, such as maintaining their basic household budget and covering their housing costs over longer-term goals that one might traditionally associate with the American Dream.

THE UNTOLD PAIN

Of all the stories being told regarding the role of consumers' Herculean efforts in holding up and growing our national economy, one of the most important stories not being told is that while our national economy continues to get stronger, our own personal economy is getting weaker. We missed the story that greater national economic resilience came at the expense of, not with, personal economic resilience.

In 2008, we as a nation watched what seemed to most of us like an otherwise healthy and financially sound bank (Lehman Brothers) collapse under the stress of a faltering economy.

The feds, in response, instituted mandatory bank health and stress tests so that we could pressure test whether a bank would be able to withstand greater pressure in more volatile economic environments.

Similarly, a medical heart stress test lets doctors know whether someone who might otherwise appear healthy has an underlying condition that might make them less resilient and vulnerable to collapse under greater stress and harsher conditions. The point is that we have ways to detect underlying conditions indicative of poor fundamental health and a lack of resilience that threaten sustainability under harsher conditions. Similar to personal and bank health and stress tests, consumers have been flashing the warning signs of an unhealthy and failing personal economy, yet this has generally gone unnoticed.

When we look at the increasing level of debt, the inability to pay for an emergency, decreasing savings, not enough in retirement, the percentage of people living paycheck to paycheck, the people working multiple jobs, the budgetary trade-offs, the people delaying retirement, the people who are unretiring, the greater worry about the impact of a layoff, and the people relocating to chase housing affordability, not their American Dream, we can clearly see the story of a lack of personal economic resilience in the face of a cumulative and collectively tougher environment.

It is a story about people afraid of one medical crisis or one emergency because they live on a tightrope. It is a story about consumers whose knees are buckling as they hold up the national economy. This is the untold story of people diverting, downsizing, and deferring their dreams of tomorrow to navigate their today.

CHAPTER 4

DISRUPTIVE SHIFTS

In addition to the historical and economic shifts we are navigating, other big contextual shifts are taking place in our lives. Devastatingly hard, impossible-to-predict, disruptive events are now happening with such regularity that they are beginning to feel like business as usual.

THE NEW NORMAL

The new dimension to our life is VUCA, which stands for *volatility, uncertainty, complexity,* and *ambiguity*. It is an acronym for our current context.

- **V:** Volatility refers to the rapid and unpredictable nature of change.
- **U:** Uncertainty highlights the lack of predictability of events and issues. You cannot use the past to predict the future.
- **C:** Complexity describes the intertwined parts, forces, and issues, making cause-and-effect relationships unclear.
- **A:** Ambiguity references the unclear cause and effect or solutions.

VUCA—NAVIGATING A NEW LIFE CONTEXT

As we think about the faster pace of change, VUCA is our new context. We did not necessarily figure our context into our lives previously, because we assumed our life context was steady and generally predictable. We got used to decades of economic growth and expansion, and within our lifetime, we expected to experience life transitions such as living on our own for the first time, marriage or starting a new long-term relationship, becoming a parent, major career change, etc. Big disruption was the exception, not the rule. Life was expected to move on a straight line, straight path, and always going one direction: forward.

Economic upheaval, our more globalized and networked world, disruptive technology, and the accelerating speed of change have profoundly altered our existence. It isn't just the fact that we're experiencing these changes that leave us so unsettled; it's also the incredible and increasing rate of these changes that leaves us feeling imbalanced.

Now, we are experiencing more and more once-in-a-generation occurrences. We are experiencing more life transitions in a given year than people used to in a lifetime. Now, with the many expansions and contractions, our life path more closely resembles an accordion that periodically squeezes us instead of the steady path upward we envisioned.

PATTERNS DISRUPTED

The pandemic was one such once-in-a-generation occurrence that completely upended almost everything about our lives, from how we worked and went to school to how we connected with our loved ones.

Work was disrupted. Universal truths were no longer true, such as when, where, and how people worked. The pandemic quickly merged and blurred our work and personal lives. There was a double-sided pressure to meet the rising expectations at work and home. On the one hand, there was pressure to do more at work, take on extra tasks, or even move into unfamiliar roles due to company pivots. On the other hand, the increased expectations of juggling more complicated home lives, especially if school-age kids were involved, meant that our lives were more fragmented than ever.

The blurring of our work and personal time was a significant source of stress. Many employees felt anxious, stressed, and emotionally drained after nearly a full year of remote work and lockdowns. Employee burnout has only gotten worse, with more than half of workers saying they felt burned out and more than two-thirds believing the feeling worsened throughout the pandemic.

The change in how and where we work has also brought greater loneliness. We are more digitally connected but less personally connected, which has deepened our sense of isolation. Employees say they spend more time in meetings but have fewer work friends.

All this results in the fact that by many measures, people are unhappier at work than they have been in years. According to Gallup's 2023 workplace report, the number of US workers who say they are angry, stressed, and disengaged is climbing. Meanwhile, a BambooHR analysis of data from more than 57,000 workers shows job satisfaction scores have fallen to their lowest point since early 2020, after a 10 percent drop this year alone.

> "I juggle two jobs, so that leaves little time or energy to socialize with my coworkers after work. Even when I am in the office, since we are not all there at the same time, I feel this strange emptiness."
> —Elliott

Formative life experiences were disrupted. For students, the pandemic disrupted their formative educational experiences, which were preparing them for work and life. Recent graduates were forced to study online during the pandemic rather than share the rites of passage of in-person high school and college experiences that previous generations had.

The college experience of earlier generations was not only the academics; it was also the friendships formed, the social gatherings, and the coming-of-age experiences and life lessons that were core to the full experience.

Young adults believe their maturity has been stunted, in what experts are calling the "pandemic skip," which essentially means that whatever age you were when the pandemic started is where you're at mentally, because those three years were wasted. Students worry about achieving their parents' milestones, especially when they have not received the same formative experiences. Consequently, they are less prepared, less socially connected, and more isolated. Just 44 percent of Gen Zers say they feel prepared for the future.

Lifestyles were disrupted. We spend significantly less time connecting with others than we did decades ago, and this trend is being felt in workplaces, schools, and homes. Nearly a third of US adults report feeling lonely at least once a week, and 10 percent say they are lonely every day. Last year, US Surgeon General Vivek Murthy declared loneliness an epidemic, highlighting the detrimental effect of social isolation on our mental and physical well-being.

A recent study sheds light on just how dangerous loneliness is. Researchers found that those who felt lonely had no one to confide in, lived alone, did not have visits from friends and family, or did not engage in weekly group activities and faced a higher risk of dying from any cause.

> Sarah, forty, lives alone in a studio apartment. To combat loneliness, she says, "I put myself out there. I introduce myself to my neighbors. I make many of my friends through fitness classes and professional networking events."

THE STATE OF EMOTIONAL WELL-BEING

Because of the constant disruptions we experience, we can sometimes feel that we live in a world that is too fragmented, too disjointed, and too noisy. This can feel tiring and exhausting and take a toll on our psyche. There is a collective emotional exhaustion because of what is going on in the background of our lives. When you're exhausted, you don't feel like doing the things that would have felt pretty normal previously. Instead, you try to make yourself do things, but the enjoyment isn't there the same way it used to be.

We are also now living with greater stress and anxiety as part of our context. So not only are we managing the VUCA context itself and the multiple disruptions in our life and work, but we now also need to manage the stress and anxiety caused by this volatile and uncertain context.

Prior to this, we were able to live with a somewhat greater level of predictability and stability, which created more psychological safety. In the past, our ability to plan for the future allowed us to not completely eliminate but to mitigate threats. Now, the threats we face are pervasive. We therefore live with constant worry. With this constant uncertainty and the context of a lack of psychological safety, worry is high. Whether we worry about existential threats, national threats, or personal or economic threats, our sense of survival is threatened. One impact of VUCA is that stress is now added to our lives, because as human beings, we are hardwired to avoid uncertainty and ambiguity.

STRESS AND WELL-BEING

There has been a global rise in stress, sadness, physical pain, worry, and anger. Stress has been rising for the past decade. Globally, it's been a slow, steady, fifteen-year march of rising stress. Stress and the resulting burnout have been called the "health epidemic of the 21st century" by the World Health Organization.

Although the pandemic officially ended on May 11, 2023, psychologists with the American Psychological Association say that we are obscuring, and therefore not sufficiently addressing, the post-traumatic effects that have altered our mental and physical health. In their survey data, APA psychologists widely agree there is mounting evidence that our society is experiencing the psychological impacts of collective trauma. Widespread trauma has not been limited to the pandemic, and cumulatively, it all weighs on the collective consciousness of Americans.

The data suggests the long-term stress sustained since the COVID-19 pandemic began has had a significant impact on well-being, evidenced by an increase in chronic illnesses. Psychological science has revealed that long-term stress creates risks for a variety of mental health

> Coping with long-term stress requires a different set of skills than adjusting to temporary stressors, as stress puts the body on high alert, and ongoing stress can accumulate, causing inflammation, wearing on the immune system, and increasing the risk of a host of ailments, including digestive issues, heart disease, weight gain, and stroke.

challenges, may make us feel more sensitive even to daily hassles, can have broader impacts on our general life outlook and goals, and affects the body's physiological response to stressors in ways that have notable implications for our physical health. Coping with long-term stress requires a different set of skills than adjusting to temporary stressors, as stress puts the body on high alert, and ongoing stress can accumulate, causing inflammation, wearing on the immune system, and increasing the risk of a host of ailments, including digestive issues, heart disease, weight gain, and stroke.

A CUMULATIVE, COLLECTIVE, AND CASCADING EXPERIENCE

We used to think about trauma, grief, and our mental health and well-being as being an individual phenomenon. Discussions of mental health were about how we as individuals were experiencing our world, coping with our individual trauma, and hopefully growing as individuals. But now, the disruptions we are experiencing—the trauma, grief, loneliness, and stress—are all part of a shared human experience, not an individual one.

So, we are now dealing with cascading and collective trauma. Cascading and collective trauma are "chronic events with an ambiguous endpoint. We do not know how bad things will get, nor when recovery can truly begin." All these disruptive changes and physical and emotional threats we face can lead to loss and grief. Today, we grieve the loss of normalcy. We grieve the loss of our normal routines and the world as we knew it. This is called "collective grief." We grieve the loss of the future that we had anticipated, which is now shrouded in uncertainty. This is called "anticipatory loss." Some of us have lost so many things that we can't even put a finger on the cause of our grief. This is called "ambiguous loss." Many of us have lost so much so quickly that we haven't even had time to grieve what we've lost. We are experiencing stress and grief at a level we have never known.

The impact of our trauma and grief feels greater each time because we have a lower capacity to respond effectively, and we haven't had enough time to recover from the last thing. We may be weathering the same storm of traumas, but we're all managing it slightly differently. Trauma shows up in our bodies, and it can affect us in unseen ways.

One experience that demonstrates how collective our experience of well-being is occurred when Elmo, one of Sesame Street's favorite characters, checked in on social media to ask people, "How is everybody doing?" The responses to Elmo's post became a viral sensation, with just over two hundred million views. Many made clear in the comments that they were not doing so well. Some cited being laid off, feeling tired, or noting they're "depressed and broke."

According to Sesame Workshop's executive vice president, chief marketing and brand officer, no one anticipated how deeply this particular question would resonate. At first glance, it might have looked like a run-of-the-mill social media check-in: "How is everybody doing?" But the message came from Elmo, the Muppet known for his capacity to care, so people unburdened themselves. "Elmo, I'm having a rough time. Love you, though," one Instagram user wrote. Elmo's response was simple and expressed what we all hope those who care about us would say: "Elmo hopes you doing okay. Elmo loves you today and every day."

It is also our response to anyone who in this moment needs to hear this message:

We hope you're doing okay. You are loved today and every day.

5

CHAPTER 5

PARADIGM SHIFTS

A central part of the old Mastery Blueprint was the carrot that was supposed to be at the end—happiness. However, for many who climb the ladder to success, one of the biggest secrets they find hard to acknowledge is that the happiness they thought would come packaged along with their success is often not there.

THE STATE OF HAPPINESS

> "From a young age, I was taught that success means getting good grades, going to a good school, and getting a good-paying job. And that's exactly what I did, but I wasn't any happier than when I started. I realized that I had spent all that time working toward someone else's definition of success."
> —Adrian

More money and a larger lifestyle were supposed to make us happier, but instead, many are left wondering why, after all the sacrifice, it was not what they thought it would be. They now wonder if this is all there is. Why are they still feeling unfulfilled? What was wrong with them such that after all the studying, training, pain, sacrifice, and missed family events, they still felt every bit as trapped by their lives as they'd felt when they were still struggling to make it? But in fact, they are not alone. Happiness has been in decline for the last several decades.

PRIORITIES WERE SHIFTED

The pandemic shifted millions of workers from physical to virtual workplaces, one effect of which was to weaken the hold jobs had on our psyches. For many people, the pandemic was the great interrupter that allowed us to think about our lives differently. There was a new urgency to think about how we use our time and to prioritize our entire lives, not just how we work.

The pandemic was a crisis that forced us to reevaluate so many of the assumptions that formed the basis of our lives. For many people, the pandemic served as a giant pause button that forced people to slow down and evaluate their lives and how they were spending their time.

Many people began questioning the purpose of their jobs and the role work should play in their lives. People were no longer willing to trade their well-being for hustle culture. There was a renewed focus on relationships, and people were no longer willing to give in to the idea that work itself was the pathway to happiness.

The impact of all the world's stressors and threats exacted such a huge toll on our lives that we needed to prioritize our mental health and well-being. This was a huge departure from how we operated before, when we simply prioritized our job and assumed that health and happiness would follow. We are now thinking about our lives differently, and as a result, there is an awakening and new urgency to prioritize our entire lives, not just our work.

Looking to be more present in their own lives, people started thinking not only about what they were striving for but also about what they were missing: time with family and friends, time to relax, and time for the things and the experiences that mattered to them. As individuals, we shifted our life priorities and aligned our lives not only with our jobs but also with our values and priorities as whole people.

We became unwilling to defer and wait for happiness. Work was no longer just the main priority at all costs. There was an awareness of the fragility of life and the importance of now. There was an evaluation of how we were spending our time and the fact that many of us were starving for genuine, deep, soul-touching intimacy in the context of decreasing connections with others. A new life expectation arose. No longer do we wait for happiness and fulfillment. We have a new goalpost that is about not just success but the quality of our lives each and every single day. No more "I'll be happy when …" We want to feel progress and fulfillment along the way.

THE PARADIGM SHIFT: WHAT WE REALLY WANT

Years after the pandemic upended American life, we have shifted our paradigm and developed a new definition of success. Recent surveys have highlighted our new life priorities—what we really want.

1. "Forget being rich; I just want to be comfortable."

    Contrary to our old notions of success being a six-figure salary or achieving millionaire status, most Americans no longer think they need a specific number or income level to achieve financial success. So, it isn't so much about reaching a lofty net worth in the future. It is about living comfortably.

    A comfortable life for many now means:

- Being able to afford to pay day-to-day expenses in order to meet life's demands without worrying about finances, such as being able to pay bills on time and being debt-free.
- Being able to enjoy life and small luxuries on a daily basis, like a cup of coffee, without worry.
- Being able to put money into savings.

2. "I want to be optimistic about my career prospects, to have a decent salary, and to do work that does some good in the world."

    While many Americans say that having a job they love is an important factor in financial happiness, a majority of people across all generations say they work to live rather than live to work and are looking for a clear separation between their work and life. A vast majority believe a better work-life balance would bring them more happiness.

3. "I want my life to reflect who I truly am. I want to feel like I'm making a significant contribution and leaving a legacy in a way that matters to me."

    For many people, the American Dream has become more of a personal dream of achieving the things that matter to them most rather than a dream of achieving a specific marker of financial success. Their priorities for success are more about a meaningful life, which includes being able to do work that has a positive impact on other people, enjoying their work, having a purpose in life, and being actively involved in their community.

THE AMERICAN DREAM AND BLUEPRINT REVISITED

Collectively, the historical, economic, and disruptive shifts, along with the transformational paradigm shift that came from the pandemic, all converge to tell an important story. Success, as we've redefined it, is now more holistic than simply attaining a specific salary, a home, or a specific net worth. We are now prioritizing all aspects of our lives. The new American Dream is now personal. This paradigm shift is important because it is the basis for constructing a new life blueprint for success in this more complex world.

BACK TO THE FUTURE

Our new, more human-centered view of success echoes and brings us back to where we began—the way the American Dream was originally articulated nearly a century ago by James Truslow Adams. In 1931, he stated,

> "The American Dream that has lured tens of millions of all nations to our shores in the past century has not been a dream of merely material plenty, though that has doubtlessly counted heavily."

> As mentioned earlier, "it has been a dream of being able to grow to fullest development as man and woman, unhampered by the barriers which had slowly been erected in the older civilizations, unrepressed by social orders which had developed for the benefit of classes rather than for the simple human being of any and every class."

Nearly a century later, we have returned to this original vision of a successful life.

WHAT WE ALL KNOW

Success and ambition are no longer just about power and work achievement. Our VUCA world has left us feeling vulnerable, particularly in our careers, finances, mental health, and lifestyle. People are no longer just striving to climb the corporate ladder. We want to be ambitious in ways that matter to us and feel solid and sustainable, regardless of the constant headwinds we face in this fast-changing world.

This new view of success fundamentally changes how we view life and work and our definitions of success. What we now search for is a life that merges our personal and professional dreams of wealth as we personally define them, our health and well-being, and our happiness.

We want to make enough to live comfortably, having enough to afford a little daily luxury. In this more volatile world, we want the peace of mind that we will be able to weather the storms we see and the upcoming storms we don't see so that we can live our own definition of our highest and fullest. This new view might appear to some as though people are searching for less—that they are less ambitious—when in fact they are really searching for more. More meaning, more relationships, more experiences, more memories, more ... life.

THE CHALLENGE

The challenge is that we are pushed and pulled simultaneously. The pull is toward the fulfillment and meaning we desire. The push is toward the financial security of our jobs and the requirements we must fulfill to keep them. The question is no longer about how to make a living; it is about how to control our own destiny and how to make a life with meaning and purpose. To get there, we need new solutions for working, living, and leading. This is what we all want; we're just not sure how to get there.

Whether it is about the value of education in these times, the role of work in our lives, the best way to get ahead, what success really means, how to prioritize broader life goals, or whether or not retirement is out of reach, these pain points all speak to the fact that we are standing in a moment where the old American Dream and blueprint no longer guide us toward our new view of success, but we haven't yet defined the new life blueprint and, just as importantly, the new path and guidance to get us there in these uncertain times.

The vacuum that has emerged from the crumbling of our old blueprint is being felt deeply. But even in this moment of pain and uncertainty, ultimately our new vision of success resonates and guides us from within because of what we all know. We all know that we search for something deeper, more valuable inside ourselves, but we get lost in our lives and lost in the day-to-day hurdles as we reach for happiness. It resonates because it articulates what we all aspire to: a life well lived.

PART 2

MEETING THE MOMENT

THE INNOVATOR BLUEPRINT

6

CHAPTER 6

OVERVIEW AND GUIDE

Though we have a new way to redefine success and our goals, we do not know how to prepare ourselves for success in this new world. We have seen that education does not have the same return on investment that it did in the past. We also do not know how to navigate toward success, as the career ladders, paths, and social contracts that we relied upon in the past are gone.

We also have never needed to learn how to lead and manage our lives so we can grow sustainably and progress toward our dreams in uncertainty, change, and disruption. The blueprint and rules we have followed all our lives were based on the 20th century's more stable, predictable industrial economy and context, not the more complex digital, globalized, and fast-changing context in which we currently live.

WHAT IS THE NEW AMERICAN DREAM?

Our new dream isn't about reaching a specific salary or net worth. It is no longer a number. It now has a lot to do with meeting life's demands and enjoying life on a daily basis. In other words, our new definition of success lies at the intersection of health, happiness, and wealth.

We are looking to be healthy personally and economically so that we are resilient. We are looking for happiness through a sustainable quality of life, and we are looking to be wealthy as defined by having a sustainable standard of living. While this is how we now define a life well lived, we currently have no blueprint that guides us to our new definition of success.

THE OLD GAME OF LIFE

The way we used to play the game of life was that we studied hard for the first couple of decades so that we could work hard for the next several decades. We were then supposed to arrive at a place called "success," earning happiness and fulfillment from that hard work. We were then supposed to be able to retire securely for the remaining decades of our lives.

We were reasonably assured that this path would work if we put in the hard work required. With continued effort, our standard of living and quality of life would lift, and we would not go backward, because our education had created a floor and insulator for us.

Our future was taken care of for us. Life infrastructure and scaffolding were provided for us. From the previously clear education-to-career paths in stable industries to the long-term stability with defined retirement benefits, we were able to work toward some basic level of stability and security and live a life with built-in infrastructure that helped us stay sustainable.

We had a less challenging short-term navigation context. We did not live in a context of constant change and disruption, so the load was not as cumulatively or collectively heavy for such a prolonged period of time. The backdrop of our lives was decades of economic growth and expansion, and within our lifetime, we expected life transitions such as living on our own for the first time, marriage or starting a new long-term relationship, becoming a parent, having a major career change, etc. Big disruption was the exception, not the rule. Life was expected to move on a straight line, straight path, and always going one direction: forward.

WHAT BROUGHT US HERE WON'T TAKE US THERE

In the past, hard work was rewarded with greater security. The longer you worked, the more stability and predictability you built for the future. At its core, the old Mastery Blueprint was based on a path with certainty.

But now, for the first time in our history, rather than adapting to an existing, steady-state context, we need to adapt to change in a constantly shifting context. So, our goal is not to develop a blueprint to navigate one path. Our new goal must be to respond to our constantly shifting context by developing a new life blueprint that will be able to move with the times while retaining core stability.

In other words, our goal is not to adapt ourselves to a static blueprint that guides us to a static goal. Our new blueprint must provide a broad frame that allows us to constantly adapt, grow, thrive, and become sustainable in our new context of uncertainty.

The old Mastery Blueprint was about mastering the known. One career, one job, one employer, one career ladder. The assumptions that underpinned the old mastery paradigm are no longer valid. We need to create a new paradigm based on the assumptions of this new normal to help us navigate and succeed sustainably in our more complex world. So, we must learn to navigate in uncertainty, not wait for certainty. We therefore need a new blueprint for living and working through times of change, disruption, and uncertainty.

The new context has given rise to a new kind of blueprint. We have reimagined the old 20th century Mastery Blueprint and have created a new 21st century Innovator Blueprint that presents the five critical paradigm shifts we all must know to shift from obsolete rules and assumptions to what we now must know to be successful today and in the future, based on our context of change and disruption. This is a new blueprint for growth. This is a new blueprint for navigating, succeeding, and thriving in uncertainty. Ultimately, it is a blueprint for a life well lived.

INTRODUCTION TO THE NEW LIFE BLUEPRINT AND ROAD MAP

Our current understanding of how to lead our lives comes from understanding life in a steady-state context, not a constantly shifting context. Disruption, however, requires a shift in our paradigm altogether.

THE GAP

This new context of complexity has rendered what we understood about the path to success insufficient and, in some cases, obsolete. Currently, we have neither the tools nor the understanding to view life in a disruptive context.

FIGURE 6.1: CONE OF POSSIBILITIES

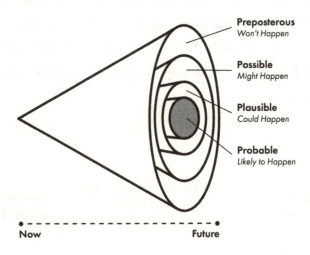

The Cone of Possibilities illustrates the variety of futures that can emanate from the current moment in time. In highly disruptive environments like the one we are currently experiencing, possible and even preposterous futures become more likely.

REIMAGINING HOW WE LEAD, MANAGE, AND INNOVATE OUR LIVES IN THE 21ST CENTURY

Based on insights from fourteen disciplines, including neuroscience, economics, organizational behavior, performance psychology, business and leadership management, sports science, and human-centered design thinking, and our deep professional expertise from decades as a psychologist, leadership and performance consultant, and Wall Street executive, we have created a multidisciplinary science to bridge the gap of how we must prepare, navigate, lead, manage, and constantly innovate to sustain our success in this context of change and disruption.

Personal Leadership, Management, and Innovation is the name of our new mental, financial, career, and lifestyle framework for how to develop across the lifespan—based on the new 21st century Innovator Blueprint—by closing the gap between our old paradigm and the new one.

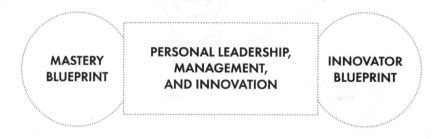

THE NEW GAME OF LIFE

Not only do we need to learn to respond to disruption; we also need to learn to play the game of life in a completely different way.

In the old game of life, we were taught to play the game one way—to climb the ladder to get us to success. But the rules of the game have changed. The new game now requires the same high level of skills in all of us that we used to expect only of athletes and CEOs. Now we all need to train the same way. We need to prepare differently, train differently, and lead and manage ourselves differently.

To win the new game of life, we now need to learn how to play five games, not just one, to perform at the elite level, even under greater pressure, like athletes and CEOs.

1. **FUTURE OF WORK GAME**

   We need to not just obtain a degree. We need to translate information into skills that allow us to create value in the marketplace and obtain the essential skills that are uniquely human.

2. **BUSINESS OF YOU GAME**

   We need the key literacies to self-lead and self-manage to create the Business of You Engine™ so we can succeed and thrive sustainably.

3. **LIFE FITNESS GAME**

   We must develop the key economic and personal fitnesses that will allow us to improve our well-being, maintain health, and maintain our standard and quality of living even in uncertainty.

4. **MENTAL GAME**

   We need to center being dynamic, not just being degreed. We must develop a mindset and intelligences that allow us to be more innovative, dynamic, agile, flexible, and resilient in uncertainty.

5. **LIFE NAVIGATION GAME**

   We must learn how to navigate life to become future proofed, which now includes managing constant change and uncertainty as well as a more challenging personal economy in the short run.

NOW PLAYED OVER MANY ROUNDS

We used to see life as one big game over one big round. Now, we not only need to train for performance at a higher level to navigate the world in this increased uncertainty, but because of our constantly changing lives, it is like playing a championship game that consists of many rounds.

Across the blueprints, you will learn how to get to your goal of a life well lived. To do so, you must learn to do the following:

- Lead your life to play the game in uncertainty and over multiple rounds.
- Manage not just your lifespan but your healthspan for sustainability.
- Innovate to change and adapt as you create opportunity.
- Prepare to play this new game of life.

For each of the five blueprints, we start with the old paradigm

and the gaps that have been created by that old paradigm.

We provide the key paradigm shift, new goal, and

the basics that you need to know about the new Innovator Blueprint.

We used to be able to use age and other developmental milestones and rites of passage as a way of understanding whether we were on track as we navigate life. Since we have lost our markers and rites of passage to let us know whether or not we are on track, our four-stage road map model allows you to determine if you are on track.

Our road maps move you from the first level, which is living on a tightrope in the old paradigm,

to basic foundational health in a new paradigm

to building the capacity for higher performance to respond to more challenging situations and environments

to playing the game like an elite performer in order to win your constantly changing game throughout your life.

7

CHAPTER 7

BLUEPRINT 1

FROM MATERIAL PLENTY TO HEALTH, WEALTH, AND HAPPINESS

Often people attempt to live their lives backward. They try to have more things or more money in order to do more of what they want so that they will be happier. The way it actually works is the reverse. You must first be who you really are and then do what you need to do in order to have what you want.
—MARGARET YOUNG

THE MASTERY BLUEPRINT

In the past, we believed that happiness would come only after we'd checked off the things on our list, so there were always things we needed to do to get to the place called "happy." For example, "I'll be happy when I get the dream job ... I get married ... I get a raise." Our lives became a checklist for success and happiness: Dream job by twenty-five? Check. Married by thirty? Check. Dream home by thirty? Check.

THE NEW LIFE BLUEPRINT

WHAT WE LEARNED

For decades, we always thought that once we achieved success in our careers, we were supposed to be happy and fulfilled. The assumption was that there would be a reward called "happiness," but that reward was always in the future. That was the old path.

 ## CONTEXT MATTERS

We assumed that as we settled into our lives and careers, with enough hard work, in time, we would eventually arrive at the place we called "happiness." The trap was believing that there was some magical destination. We think happiness comes only after we've checked off the things on our list in order to get to happy—things we need to do, things we need to accomplish, things we need to buy, and milestones we need to reach. We'd all been seduced into believing that there was a magical destination of happiness and fulfillment at the end. And even more, we believed that once we got there, it would justify all the pain and sacrifice and *not living* that it required along the way.

SHIFT IN LIFE PRIORITIES

With the many world shifts we have endured, we changed our consciousness from emptying ourselves to succeed to a consciousness that prioritized our full-life goals. It was no longer about acquisition as a marker of success; it was now about more moments, more health, more sustainability.

WHAT WE WANT

We are now searching for ways to integrate our increasingly disjointed lives to bring more fulfillment. We are prioritizing our health and happiness and framing the ability to have enough to sustain the standard and quality of our lives as our new American Dream, not simply how much money we make.

SHIFT PARADIGM FROM THIS ...

TO THIS:

THE INNOVATOR BLUEPRINT

SUCCESS REDEFINED

We must redefine success from a narrow focus on career ambition to a broader focus on our simultaneous health, wealth, and happiness. This means human success is now defined as better overall well-being and a better quality- and standard-of-life in addition to our broader goals of success.

 **NEW GOAL**

This kind of success requires us to move beyond our old ideas of success and redefine success and ambition in a more holistic way. It also requires a new paradigm, new habits, and new skills as we navigate the shifts required to live, lead, and lift higher.

BLUEPRINT 1: FROM MATERIAL PLENTY TO HEALTH, WEALTH, AND HAPPINESS

 THE BASICS

It is not just about the quantity of our life but also the quality of our life. In other words, it is not just about how many years we live or our material wealth—it is also about the quality of our life experiences. The new success goes beyond position and power to create a lifestyle in the here and now that includes both our bigger goals for achieving a sense of meaning and fulfillment and our right-now goals for things that bring us joy and happiness and increase our overall sense of well-being. This integrated view of success must reflect what it means to live in fulfillment today rather than chasing it tomorrow.

THE HEALTH, WEALTH, AND HAPPINESS ROAD MAP

 **LEVEL 1**

CAREER INTELLIGENCE

Our old definition of success got us to a place that was only about the quantity of our lives.

We used to travel the road of success by emptying ourselves first, and then we would hope that happiness and fulfillment would be at the end.

It is easy to get caught in the trap of measuring your success by your job title or the attainment of a certain financial threshold, like making $100,000 annually. Success in this view is also power by association—whom you associate with—as well as power as defined by things you have plus power based on what you do and achieve.

The conflict at the root of the pain so many of us feel right now is a push-pull dilemma—the pull toward personal happiness, fulfillment, and meaning and the push toward the financial security we need for daily survival. We struggle every day to move toward our goal of our broader dreams, which is ultimately about freedom and independence. Survival of the moment takes perseverance but at great cost, because we often go missing and become disengaged in our own lives. The simultaneous push-pull is leading many to feel trapped in their own lives.

We go through life being career intelligent—in other words, seeing ourselves through a job title or career. We wrap ourselves and our lives around the awareness of ourselves from the choices we made when we were eighteen. We define ourselves first by declaring our college major and then our first job. But here's the problem: the more we live, the more we end up burying and filtering our sense of who we are outside these markers of success.

When we set out to build successful careers by developing skills that allow us to provide for ourselves and our families, those skills are not necessarily the ones we care most deeply about. But because we usually interpret our lives through the narrow lens of the skills we have built up, it later becomes difficult for us to see ourselves without the filter of what we have thus far been rewarded for. Our identities and our sense of purpose are too closely tied to our employer, which in turn gives other people too much power to define our overall happiness.

Whether it's for financial security or social rewards and acceptance, we often lose sight of what is most true about us. We stop connecting—or even trying to connect—to our true sense of who we are because of our daily obligations. We don't even realize we are trading away things that really mean something to us because we haven't put the right value on those things in the first place.

If we never even attempt to find our center of gravity, we end up feeling like we are drifting in the wind—chasing a bunch of goals that shift and change—because there's no big picture for our lives. We then realize the skills and strategies we learned that brought us to this place no longer seem to take us where we really want to go because of the constant waves of change coming at us.

If we do connect with our inner compass at some point but later bury it, we live with constant pain and yearning for what we lost because we never learned who we were standing still—without the titles and all the other things we use as stand-ins for who we really are.

Without a bigger vision for our lives, we live without joy. It feels as if we are just existing. There are no highs as we go through the motions each day to get to what is meaningful to us in the long run without knowing what to do in the here and now. This cycle leaves us with the yearning to do what matters to us without knowing how to pay the bills today. Even without being able to name it exactly, we usually know that something is off. Sometimes, the feeling is vague; we know we're confused and that something is just not right. Other times, it's too painful to ignore and feels like we're in crisis.

LEVEL 2

PERSONAL INTELLIGENCE

To get to our new definition of success, we are first going to learn to be who we really are and *then* learn to do what we need to do in order to have what we really want to have. That starts with defining what success and happiness mean to you based on your bigger vision for your life. It represents what you deeply care about, what you feel is important, and what gives meaning to your existence. This is how you want to lead your life based on who you really are. Sounds simple enough, except for this ...

We are often told to write vision and purpose statements when trying to find a clearer direction in life. While that *sounds* good, it can be an exercise in frustration. When we don't know our bigger vision or how to figure it out, we just end up putting words on paper that are lost and forgotten as quickly as they are written. Most of us have either not discovered or have deeply buried who we really are.

We have no idea how to view our lives without all the filters, much less how to figure out our bigger vision and purpose. Beautifully crafted statements may sound good, but ultimately they go nowhere. We should first address the root cause of the problem—the disconnection from ourselves because we are career intelligent but not personally intelligent.

Let's take a different perspective on this important *Where to?* question so we can see ourselves differently. When we think about where we are going, it is usually through the lens of our skills and competencies *in our careers*. We need first to free ourselves of this narrow perspective, because it will lead us to a vision that's too limited.

LIFE LOCATORS

Lifting from a strong and clear center of gravity is critical physically, in life, and professionally.

Understanding your core: What do you love at your core? What are the things that engage you in life? Your core values and core strengths are critical to understand. These are all part of your core center of gravity, because people can neither give you these things nor take them away from you. These are fundamental to you.

> It is key to have an awareness of your passions and what you value, what fulfills you psychically. What is most natural to you?

It is key to have an awareness of your passions and what you value, what fulfills you psychically. What is most natural to you? What are the things that mean something to you? *Why* do those things mean something to you, and what do you just naturally want to do that brings you to being one with yourself? Knowing these things is what is already guiding your life—it is your true north and helps to give your life a sense of direction even without your knowing it. These are all life locators for the quality of your life experiences that will animate your path along the way.

WHY PERSONAL INTELLIGENCE MATTERS

When we develop high personal intelligence, we are also developing the whole person—the entire authentic human being. When we lack personal intelligence, we end up, by default, developing a persona—

the stand-in for who we are. We therefore end up going through life playing a series of roles. We play the roles that please others personally and that we get rewarded for professionally in order to attain what we think we want. What ends up happening is that we are an actor in our own life. The only difference is that while an actor knows it is a part they are playing, we over time no longer know who the real person is behind the persona.

THE PARADOX OF SUCCESS: LIVING IN SMALL SPACES

"Mind the gap" is a phrase first used in the late 1960s by the London Underground subway train system. It is a warning to train passengers to take caution while crossing the gap between the train door and the station platform and is now widely used in transit systems globally. It is a reminder that even though the train pulls into the station, you won't get to your destination unless you "mind the gap."

Although we may have learned to heed the warnings to "mind the gap" when we are stepping out of a train, for some reason we don't "mind the gap" in our own lives. We falsely assume that, as we settle into our lives and careers and eventually arrive at the station we call success, this arrival will be both the necessary and sufficient condition for getting to our final destination called "happiness." For many, though, it doesn't quite work out that way.

I hear it all the time: "I'll be happy when I ... change jobs ... get the next promotion ... find the perfect mate ... make more money ... move into a bigger house ... lose ten pounds." And when it *does* happen—when the person changes jobs, gets the next promotion, finds the perfect mate, makes more money, moves into the bigger house, or loses ten pounds—the moments of happiness that were so eagerly anticipated are short lived, if they come at all, and then they are looking for the next happiness fix. Many end up asking themselves, "Why is the success I achieve not enough to make me happy?" or simply, "Why is happiness so elusive?"

And if this wasn't already bad enough, many people have the distinct feeling that despite their best efforts, their lives don't feel like they are expanding—instead, they're shrinking, getting smaller, not larger. They ask themselves, "Why do *greater* success, *bigger* titles, and *more* things only satisfy me for the moment, and why, over time, do these temporary fixes only seem to make me feel worse and not better?" What was once the promise of limitless opportunities and potential now feels like a small box that constrains them regardless of how many goals they seem to reach. They feel as though they are living in small spaces; instead of minding the gap, it is as though they are living *in* the gap.

This is no accident. People don't suddenly get pushed into the small spaces that comprise their lives. They make conscious decisions along the way that gradually constrain them, building the boxes—board by board, nail by nail—that now restrict and define them.

There are a few ways that we come to live in these small spaces.

Small Space #1: When you are living up to the expectations of others. When we are young, the answer to the question of what we want to be when we grow up seems limitless. Adulthood, in the mind of a child, is a place of freedom, of bigness in our lives. But as children, we also delight in the praise we receive from parents and teachers, and we continue seeking this praise even as adults. Somehow, by the time we get to adulthood, the vast possibilities we saw before us as children have narrowed considerably.

What went wrong?

For many, what went wrong is, in part, the relentless pressure they felt to conform to the expectations of others. When you think about your own life, perhaps you didn't have much of a choice regarding your career path because you decided you would do everything in your power to live up to the external expectations of others while you ignored pursuing your own dreams. If you think about it, we refer to this as "living up to the expectations" that others have of us, as though *their* expectations should be higher than the ones we have of *ourselves*. Perhaps when we started out, we were okay with taking on the expectations of others, and we enjoyed the praise we got for it. But as we get older, these expectations of others end up constraining us—they make us feel small and trapped in our lives, stuck in that gap in which we are living. Regardless of how successful we might be, we're often living in a small space.

Small Space #2: When you are walking the tightrope. Getting to the top professionally often means prioritizing work most of the time and, for some, all the time. The question for many becomes whether they have created an untenable way of life. They have a collection of things around them but no enjoyment. They are just sleepwalking through their lives and feeling that they are being pulled in many different directions.

For many people, by the time they are heavily into their careers, relationships, and parenthood, they start to realize that the things they thought would save them, such as the next promotion, the bigger house, and the nicer car, were only temporary fixes. And so, they end up right back where they started—empty inside. Since the happiness they are searching for is fleeting at best, they look for other ways to justify living in these small spaces.

However they arrive at living in the gap, they look to the financial rewards, promotions, and any lifestyle benefits to distract and justify becoming more disconnected in their lives. They are making deliberate trade-offs in the hope that these trade-offs will compensate for the pain and emptiness they feel inside.

> Walking the tightrope puts us in a small space in our lives, and for many, no matter how big the reward may be, it's just not worth it. Unfortunately, few of us are willing—or able—to climb down from the tightrope that we've built our lives on and decide for ourselves what is most important to us.

When your life owns you instead of you owning it, and when you go to great lengths to justify it, you're stuck in a small space.

The foundation of life success. A key foundational element of life success is knowing how to close these gaps instead of living inside these small spaces. This begins with knowing how to consciously pursue a life where we are fully engaged. Personal intelligence—a strong core sense of who you are—is the basic building block of creating a lifestyle that allows you to intentionally choose the life you desire.

 **LEVEL 3**

LIFE INTELLIGENCE

Personal intelligence is the core building block of life intelligence, which is knowing the life and lifestyle that will animate and engage you. When you are personally intelligent, you can better distinguish your life's loves, likes, wants, and needs.

NEEDS VERSUS WANTS

Most of us can distinguish between the things we need and the things we want. For our basic survival, we all *need* shelter, air, food, and water. These are nonnegotiables. However, we may want a certain style of home or prefer certain kinds of foods over others. We understand those things are our preferences but, at our core, not needs for survival.

LOVES VERSUS LIKES

While the line between needs and wants is clear, many people who lack a core sense of who they are and therefore lack personal intelligence are not able to quickly identify the difference between what they love and what they like in their lives.

The things we love in our lives are connected to the things that engage us, animate us, amplify us, and overall help us feel more of who we are by bringing us to a place of life-flow. The key is that you must first know who you are at your core in order to know what amplifies you in some exponential way, because it resonates with the core of who you already are.

The likes in our lives are the nice-to-haves, the icing on the cake, but not fundamental in some way. The things we like are often so common and commoditized that they are not specific to us. In other words, they are the latest trends that we follow. We may like some things in these moments, but when the trends move, so do our likes. The likes in our lives are fleeting. Though likes are nonspecific and fleeting and we can ultimately do without them, the problem arises when we are not personally intelligent enough to distinguish between what we like and what we love.

Most never get to the core of who they are, so they live in the world of likes and trends and wait for others to influence what they do, what they like, and how they live. When you live unconsciously, you are living by habits that are largely shaped by what is happening outside of you. Worse yet, you end up accepting these choices as things you believe you love, while they are nothing more than unconscious living shaped by things that are not core to what matters to you. You therefore end up living your life in one of four quadrants:

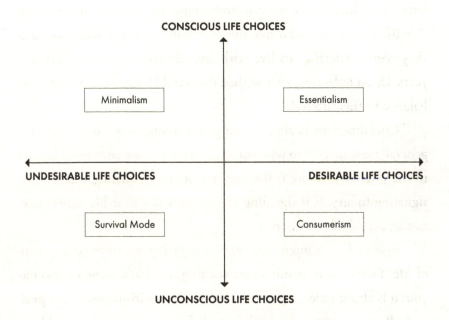

Essentialism is the foundation of life intelligence. It means making conscious life choices based on your needs and loves, not your likes and wants.

Most of us are having near-life experiences. They are near-life experiences because they are not based on anything that adds to the real and meaningful quality of life. In some cases, they only add to the quantity of life.

When we are in survival mode, we are living on such a tightrope that we are on autopilot to get through each day. It is both an unconscious and undesirable way to live, because we can see and manage only the crisis that is immediately in front of us—there is no space mentally, financially, or emotionally for anything else but to survive the moment.

Living a minimalist lifestyle is often a response to trying to get out of survival mode, or it can be a choice to live in an extremely minimalist way in the present to be fully financially independent later on in life. While we can understand the functional benefit of this lifestyle, many who live this way will say upon reflection that they regret deferring to live with any life enjoyment for so many years. Upon reflection, they wished they could have created a bit more balance in their lifestyle.

Consumerism is about having and doing more, but since it is generally not specific to who you are at the core, the emotional benefit to the pursuit of more is fleeting at best. It is signaling wealth, it is signaling luxury, is it signaling arrival, so it is a near-life experience, not an actual life experience.

Essentialism is intentionally choosing what improves your quality of life. Essentialism is not about reacting to what's going on around you; it is about reflecting on what is going on within you. It is a peak and a flow that comes from self-knowledge, bringing a continual high return. This is what makes these experiences sustainable, because they are organic as opposed to the ways in which we try to create peak experiences artificially.

Essentialism brings you to peak emotions that allow you to experience the continuity of your identity. It is consistent with who you are, your favorite memories, and a reminder of your loves.

Your life is not automated; instead, it is stimulated, because the quality of your experiences fills you up. These peak experiences help you reach the full expression of who you are.

For you to feel present, you must multiply the essence of who you are. These experiences become mutually reinforcing.

It is not about fewer or smaller. It is about having more of what is true and more of what you love. It is about living brighter. It is about filling yourself up emotionally. It is about emotional attachment and the physical representation of your story and your values. It is the highest quality of living anchored by your locators. You must find your loves versus your likes and your wants. It is about creating space for love, joy, and animation; it elicits emotional resonance, not just functionality, in life. Essentialism is about both function and emotion. What you need inside you is both emotionally and functionally important, and it is connected to what is outside of you. This is what creates the multiplicative effect.

MARRYING WHO YOU ARE WITH YOUR LIFE VISION, TALENTS, AND ECONOMIC ENGINE

Personal intelligence and life intelligence are about finding and living from your core *I Am* center of gravity. Now we must locate your core *I Can* center of gravity and connect those two in order to marry what you care about and what you do.

While the second blueprint will cover this in greater detail, you should ask yourself questions like these: What does professional engagement (not job engagement) look like for you? What are your strengths? What kinds of problems do you like to solve in the world, and how do you think you can create value?

THE NEW GAME OF LIFE

In the old blueprint, we created a life model which was, by default, centered around our career. Now, we must be properly equipped, prepared, and guided by our life and business model.

LIFE GOALS AND BUSINESS OF YOU GOALS

The Blueprint Life and Business Model Canvas™ was designed to introduce design thinking into the process of life modeling. Our canvas facilitates the creation of a Life and Business of You Road Map™ to grow and continuously innovate across your life.

BLUEPRINT LIFE AND BUSINESS OF YOU MODEL CANVAS

To achieve higher performance levels, businesses do not just operate; they have a business model that guides all their activities. The model helps to guide and navigate them to their desired destination. It is a way of operating, a philosophy, a guide, etc., as well as a method of figuring out how to make critical investments in its future.

To set ourselves up for higher performance, we also need the Life and Business Model Canvas™ to see when we are on- or off-track and to figure out what financial investments, skills, and lifestyle changes are necessary to live the life we want. The model canvas is a way of living, not a destination.

LEVEL 4

A NEW IDENTITY FOR SUSTAINABILITY

Learning to thrive in challenging environments throughout our lives will require constant preparation and upskilling as well as a next-level identity and mindset development.

Old ways of seeing ourselves and our identities as simply students, employees, and consumers do not work anymore. We must now see ourselves as innovators. By constantly introducing new methods, ideas, and processes, we can operationalize and then design and innovate throughout our lives.

The key is to arm yourself with the skills of an innovator and human-centered designer that put you at the center of your Life and Business Model Canvas and then innovate continuously throughout your life. That way, no matter what twists and turns our life takes, we always know how to chart our own course and stay on our path.

> Old ways of seeing ourselves and our identities as simply students, employees, and consumers do not work anymore. We must now see ourselves as innovators.

8

CHAPTER 8

BLUEPRINT 2

FROM CAREER LADDERS TO PLAYING ON YOUR COURT

Offense sells tickets, defense wins games, rebounding wins championships.
—PAT SUMMITT

THE MASTERY BLUEPRINT

One degree, one job, one employer for life: this was the path to success in the old Mastery Blueprint.

WHAT WE LEARNED

You funneled your career into one lane, worked for one employer, and mastered their business in the hope that their definition of success would eventually translate to success for you. You lived by a series of if-then statements: "If I do A, then B will happen." It was a very linear model for life success.

You progressed through life by propping your ladder up on your employer's wall. Your fate was determined by your employer, and the more you were paid, the more you attached your family's fate as well. You were told to exchange years of hard work on the front end for rewards on the back end, so the more you were willing to delay gratification on the front end, the larger the rewards you would later reap for that sacrifice.

The focus of attaining your dream became finding your dream job, because in the old blueprint, there were clear career paths, increased financial rewards, increased stability and security based on loyalty, and a social contract that helped build your life infrastructure in the form of health benefits and defined pensions for future retirement.

 **CONTEXT MATTERS**

The world of work has changed, so lifetime employment has vanished. Work is now transactional, with short-term agreements that are constantly up for review. No longer do we climb the company ladder. Instead, we have unclear career paths and career ladders and no social contract that rewards hard work and loyalty with greater security or the infrastructure that we need to thrive in our own lives.

BLUEPRINT 2: FROM CAREER LADDERS TO PLAYING ON YOUR COURT

Since this path to success is broken, hard work no longer guarantees success. Instead, we end up surrendering control of our fate to other people, which may not necessarily work out for us as circumstances change.

So, even if you do everything you were taught, you will likely not be building toward sustainable success; you will be building a house of cards vulnerable to crashing down with one layoff or industry collapse. In fact, the higher you climb and the more one person controls your life, the more vulnerable you will likely feel, since you will be aware that it can all come crashing down at any moment. The world of work has changed dramatically. This means that we all now have to think about and manage our careers completely differently than we used to.

SHIFT PARADIGM FROM THIS...

TO THIS:

THE INNOVATOR BLUEPRINT

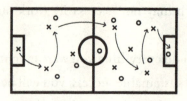

PLAYING THE GAME ON YOUR COURT

Our goal now must be to grow differently. Instead of thinking about one path, you must make a series of plays.

 NEW GOAL

The goal of your plays should be to increase choice, control, and cushion so that you can master three games of life, not just one: the Future of Work game, the Business of You game, and the Life Navigation game.

 THE BASICS

It used to be about the climb; now it needs to be about the dynamism with multiple plays we need to execute to weather the continual disruption. Since the social contract is broken, we must play the game on our own courts, not on any specific employer's court. The path to success must now be human centered. It can no longer be centered around one job or employer, so we can increase our choices, control, and cushion even in changing contexts.

BLUEPRINT 2: FROM CAREER LADDERS TO PLAYING ON YOUR COURT

THE PLAYING ON YOUR COURT ROAD MAP

HOUSE OF CARDS

We learned to play the game of life on someone else's court. We played as the talent, and our employer brought the infrastructure, so we played on their court. We played the game of life successfully by narrowing our choice into one major, selecting one career path to master one game, and then working for one employer to master their business for life.

If you do this now, if you do everything you were taught to do, you will not be building toward success. You will be building a house of cards, because you will have fewer choices over time.

The more talented you are and the more money you make, the less control you have over your life. Unsustainable growth occurs when you grow but reduce your control and choices along the way. That is why, even if you work hard and play by the rules, you still don't feel like you're winning, because you are playing the wrong game.

No more trusting that if you grind, it will eventually pay off.

No more trusting that someone else will take care of what you want.

The old social contract is gone, and the contract is now with you.

So, while you learned to play strong offense in your career during a time when the path was more predictable, now you must play a very different game of offense *and* defense to manage the short-term challenges you face—all while playing your game over several rounds. This is a new game altogether. We can no longer simply learn one way to work based on one major and hope that this will be the case for the rest of our lives. We need to learn a series of plays, a series of ways to work, and the way to navigate changing winds for both the long haul and the short run.

LEVEL 2

PLAYING THE GAME ON YOUR COURT

HOME COURT ADVANTAGE

The path to success is no longer climbing the career ladder. Now, we must lead our lives differently by playing the game on our court, not on someone else's ladder. We have a new relationship with the world of work. Since there is no longer a social contract with employers, the contract is now with ourselves. This means you play the game on your court instead of wrapping your life around a specific employer.

We must move from following predetermined paths on a career ladder that narrows our choices to leading our lives differently by playing the game on our court—by taking full charge of our skills and the many ways we can work.

THE CONTRACT IS WITH YOU

Making the contract with yourself means that you must know your own value, not just your employer's value. You can't wait for someone to define you, your value, your direction, or your worth. Your core and foundation must be solid.

CAREER SMOOTHING

The game is nonlinear. We used to see the path from school to employer to climbing the ladder as very linear. Now it is not passive or linear—it is more similar to a series of nonlinear plays from a playbook. Instead of believing that you will have one job and one career for life, you must see that the game is now going to be played over several rounds. Your road to the championship is no longer one path but several plays in your playbook for navigation that you play on *your* court. The game is now nonlinear rather than sequential and will be played over multiple rounds; it is not a one-and-done success.

This means that we no longer see success as a path through one title and one job. We will now need multiple paths and ways to work to move toward our goal. Since there is no longer one path, we need to manage our destination.

So you need to see your career as a game you must play to the championship, where you must create, innovate, and pivot over multiple rounds to win. You must center *your* goals, not just hard work for someone else. You must continue to invest in the future. While you once learned to play strong offense in a done-for-you context, you must now manage the short-term challenges and play your longer game.

In an accordion world, we need to smooth the changes with more than one income stream, not all on someone else's platform. Revise your strategy by going from one path to multiple ways to work, knowing the future of work trends, and having multiple sources of income to make a living.

CAREER CUSHIONING

Career cushioning is a way for people to feel in control of their careers even amid economic uncertainty. Essentially, it is making sure that you have a plan B, a safety net, or alternative options to your current job. Career cushioning is about being proactive and creating additional opportunities for yourself in the event of a layoff or sudden termination, therefore cushioning the shock.

LEVEL 3

GAME INTELLIGENCE

Great athletes know that their sport is not just a physical game but also a mental one. For example, having a high basketball IQ is just as important as having the physical skills to shoot, dribble, and pass. Like chess, the players who are able to think three or four moves ahead of the other players on the floor excel against their competitors to win the game.

A high basketball IQ refers to the ability to play the game instinctively and adapt to any situation that comes up. It combines technical skills, game awareness, understanding, and experience. It is the ability to keep your eyes on the court and know what's happening in all corners. It is about instinctively knowing which play to make and when. It is about playing with efficiency and adapting to changes.

Similarly, while in the previous era, we were able to bring our skills and talents to our employer and trust that the life infrastructure we needed would be taken care of. That is no longer the case. We need full game intelligence to manage our more challenging present day: we need to manage our ability to be resilient in case of setbacks; we need to manage our future; we need to manage our retirement. This means we can't just manage our careers. We need to see the full court and foster full game intelligence. So, in other words, we can't just focus on growth; we also must make plays that build our life infrastructure so that we are providing our own stability and security.

You have to be able to see all the moving parts—the events happening right now, as well as the impact your next moves will have on the future. You need to know your drivers of success and diverse ways to get there. This is the multidimensional thinking you need to perform, even beyond having the necessary skills to grow your career.

Operating with full game intelligence is knowing the following:

1. The Future of Work game
2. The Business of You game
3. The Life Navigation game

THE FUTURE OF WORK GAME PLAYBOOK

Ways to make a play. You have to know the many plays you can make on the court. You need to gain more control over your time and destiny. There is no perfect one-size-fits-all solution for how we can or should work. The key is to broaden your understanding of the choices available to you and create a playbook with multiple options: the paths that best suit you and that play to your strengths. Here are a few ways to leverage your skills to create full-time, part-time, or side-gig options.

Service-Based Businesses

In service-based businesses, customers purchase your time and skills by engaging with you in a one-on-one relationship. So, whether it is a digital marketing company, an accounting agency, food catering, a plumbing company, or a hair salon, these services exist to help people who don't have the time, knowledge, or skills to complete the tasks themselves.

Consulting-Based Businesses

With a consulting-based business, like a service-based business, you have a direct relationship with your clients. However, with a consulting-based business, instead of providing a service, consultants and coaches leverage their expertise to help clients solve their problems and achieve their goals.

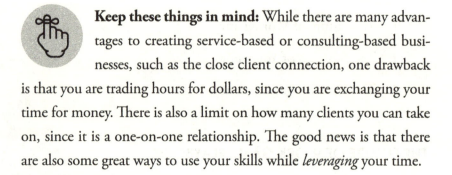

Keep these things in mind: While there are many advantages to creating service-based or consulting-based businesses, such as the close client connection, one drawback is that you are trading hours for dollars, since you are exchanging your time for money. There is also a limit on how many clients you can take on, since it is a one-on-one relationship. The good news is that there are also some great ways to use your skills while *leveraging* your time.

Product-Based Businesses

Product-based businesses deliver physical, tangible products. You can sell through your own channels or other marketplaces. As you brainstorm ideas for the kinds of products you can sell, also remember to think about your interests and what you like to do for fun and use those as ways you can create a living.

Information-Based Businesses

While consultants and coaches work one on one with their clients, information-based businesses allow you to share your expertise and information in ways that leverage your time. Like other skill- or expertise-based businesses, information-based businesses are aligned around a common problem. For example, you can be an author, a blogger, or a podcaster.

Beware—while it's easier than it's ever been to start your own business, it is not truly your own if it relies on another company or platform for audience or customers. If the fate of your business can change with algorithm updates you do not control, pricing structures you do not control, or anything else you do not control, you could be building an unpredictable business that leaves you vulnerable instead of a sustainable business.

Small Businesses

You can work out of your home with most of the previous businesses discussed. You are also the business. You are trading or leveraging your time, products, and expertise. When you disappear, so does the business. Another option is not just to create a job for yourself but to create a business with systems, processes, and staff in place to deliver a product or service.

Working inside a Company

The importance of knowing what value you add and using it to your advantage is not just for those who are self-employed. If you work for an employer, you should always see yourself as an intrapreneur. An intrapreneur is someone who adopts the same mindset as entrepreneurs, but the difference is that they work inside an organization, not for themselves. Intrapreneurs try to make themselves invaluable by constantly identifying gaps, looking for opportunities, and finding ways to innovate inside their organization.

SKILLS ARE THE NEW CURRENCY

Skills are the new currency that can position us for the future of work and will position us for success regardless of the context.

> Whether you are a new graduate trying to figure out how to get a leg up in your career or you're a midcareer professional looking to secure your next promotion, you might be wondering what the most important skills are that you need to help you get where you want to go. While it's of course important for you to develop your industry-specific or hard skills, it turns out that what's just as critical to your success are your soft or essential skills.

Soft skills are how you function in the workplace and interact with others. And while they're not easily taught in a classroom or measured, they are key skills that we all need to have. Additionally, in our more globalized, fast-changing work environment, there is now an additional premium on the kinds of essential and uniquely human skills that allow you to keep pace with the future of work.

ABILITY TO LEARN

We'll begin with the ability to learn, because it is arguably the most important 21st century skill you will need to succeed. Alvin Toffler said, "The illiterate of the 21st century will not be those who cannot read and write, but those who cannot learn, unlearn, and relearn." That's because in an environment where new skills emerge as fast as others fade in importance, success is less about what you already know and more about adapting your skills by growing and expanding your knowledge base so you can use new information to respond to whatever is happening.

AGILITY

As the work landscape shifts, learning to be agile is a critical skill, as yesterday's solutions do not solve tomorrow's problems. At the heart of being agile is shifting gears when the context calls for it and responding accordingly to the needs of your workplace, clients, or industry trends.

COLLABORATION

In our increasingly hyperconnected world, we're no longer expected to work just as individuals or in silos. Our projects have become more complex, so the ability to work effectively as part of a team has also grown in importance. Given the increasing global nature of our work, your ability to collaborate, share knowledge, and contribute to teams that can capitalize on diversity of thinking and perspective in ways that everyone can benefit and drive to the shared outcomes is key.

VERBAL COMMUNICATION

Advancing in your career is not based just on what you do. There's a good chance that at some point in your career, you'll have to speak confidently so you can sell others on your ideas, products, or services. Whether you need to explain your value when you are being considered for a promotion, present part of a team project, or speak on stage, you need to be able to communicate well and convey strong, persuasive ideas.

WRITTEN COMMUNICATION

We live in an era of tweets and sound bites, but good written communication skills still matter when it comes to your career. Whether you are sending professional emails, communicating with a client, trying to deliver a coherent business plan, or anything in between, you should be able to communicate quickly, accurately, and effectively.

EMPATHY

The ability to empathize with others—that is, trying to see things from their perspective by understanding their emotions and reactions—is a fundamental part of how we interact with one another. Empathy allows you to communicate genuinely and authentically with others, because even in instances when you disagree with your coworkers on elements of a work project, for example, empathy allows you to demonstrate to others that they are seen and heard.

CREATIVITY

Creativity is a key skill we need, because in our fast-changing times, employers value employees who can look beyond the present and imagine future possibilities for their company. Creative workers are those who ask *why*. They question, they are curious, and in so doing, they develop new ideas and solutions.

PROBLEM-SOLVING

How often do you find yourself going beyond your immediate job as assigned and instead using more knowledge, facts, and data to see gaps and solve problems? Being a good problem solver is important because employers value people who can work through problems on their own or as an effective member of a team by defining the issues, brainstorming alternatives, sharing thoughts, and then making good decisions.

LEADERSHIP

The importance of building the right culture at companies cannot be overstated, so having the skills to be able to coach, empower, and motivate those around you to do their best work is highly valued for success.

NEGOTIATION

Whether you're participating in salary discussions, finalizing a deal with a client, or trying to find common ground with your teammates during a project, effective negotiation skills are extremely important. Being a good negotiator allows you to achieve important goals and build, maintain, and improve relationships, which is a very important part of being successful in your career.

CAREER SHIFTING

While we no longer have the same expectations for staying at our jobs for a lifetime, we should also avoid the other extreme of moving from one thing to the next with no larger purpose or way to connect our moves together.

Career shifting is when you take your bigger vision, talents, strengths, and skills and use these rather than your job title as a basis for moving from one opportunity to the next. Shifting means that even when you are making a series of moves, some things will remain consistent or essentially true about you to help connect the moves so you do not just drift along aimlessly. Let me give you an example of what I mean.

After several years of being a practicing clinical psychologist, I took my talents and skills to work in a global research and best practices firm for companies and their executives. My first role was in new business development for corporate clientele.

You might be wondering (as many did) why a psychologist would consider making such a big move and whether it was a career drift versus a shift. But I was able to identify and use a few key transferrable skills that allowed me to make a smooth transition from being a practicing psychologist to working in corporate consultative sales.

Psychologists are known for being really good listeners. In fact, we call it being able to listen with the third ear—listening for the deeper layers in a conversation and hearing what is not being directly said. At the same time, what is usually the biggest complaint people have about salespeople? The complaint is that they don't listen well because they are too busy trying to sell you on their product or service.

So, I positioned myself when I made my career transition not just as a psychologist but as the best listener they could ever hire. In case you want to know how that career shift turned out for me, I ended up setting a company record for how much business I generated that year. Every position I have held or created from my playbook since then has always been an offshoot of my key talents and skills that I can transfer to seemingly very different kinds of experiences. And just as importantly, they all are ways for me to gain experiences that help me move closer to my bigger vision.

CAREER STRATEGY: ALWAYS IN THE JOB MARKET

You should be in the job market right now, and it has nothing to do with how happy you are or are not in your current job. The world of work has changed dramatically, and we no longer expect to have one job for life. Now, we all have to think about and manage our careers completely differently than we used to.

The first rule is that you now must see yourself as the boss of your own career. This is true whether you work for someone else or for yourself. If you are self-employed, you are an entrepreneur, but if you work for someone else, you are an intrapreneur. Here is what that means.

You need to always consider yourself in the job market and be open to potential new opportunities: no more waiting for someone else to decide how your career progresses; no more waiting to be in the job market only when you are unhappy or when you are forced to job search.

The second rule is that you can no longer just think about getting your next job. Instead, you need to envision having more choices and more control over your life by thinking about how to future-proof yourself with your own career playbook that always keeps you in the game and positions you for success in good times and in not-so-good times.

Here is how you create your own career strategy playbook:

- You need to be clear on and *set goals based on your bigger vision for your life*. Here is what happens at the beginning of each year. You look at your life and your job, and you decide whether or not you like your job. If not, should you look for another job? Nothing wrong with that, but the better question is this: "Am I making progress on my bigger life vision, and is this job helping me move in that direction?" This means you need to know what success is in the long run for you and not just for this moment.

- Once you know your big picture, you need to have as many ways to get there as you possibly can so you can always recover from a setback, move on to a better opportunity, or create your own opportunity. This means *you can't just see yourself as nothing more than a job title*. Instead, you need to see yourself as the *why* behind what you do. What are you really after?

    Here's an example of what I mean by that. My first career was as a practicing clinical psychologist. But when I changed my awareness of myself from "I am a psychologist" to my why—"I am a problem solver"—that switch opened up ways for me to be a problem solver in different industries and sectors with people, teams, executives, companies, and organizations, not just ways to be a psychologist.

- The next step in creating your playbook is to know your unique advantage. How do you *stand apart* from everyone else? Ask yourself two questions to figure this out.

    "What are my unique gifts and talents that, when I am in the zone, set me apart from everyone else?"

Once you know that, turn the mirror the other way and ask yourself this: "What is not only meaningful to me, but *what value do I add, what problems do I solve* where I work (or for my clients if I work for myself)?" You have to know your value—always.

- You now need to create more ways to make your plays. Once you no longer see yourself as a title and you know your unique advantage, you can begin to search for many roles based on your *why* and what sets you apart—your unique advantage. When we go to school, we are taught one way to work—for someone else. But you should also consider ways to be self-employed, like having a side gig or starting your own business, and even ways to combine plays.

    By now, we've all learned about the power of diversifying our financial investment portfolio. The same rule applies here. The investment in yourself is that you should always have at least five ways to make a play that would be in keeping with your bigger view of success in your career.

- We know life moves quickly, and it's almost impossible to keep track of all the opportunities that might be out there and available for you to consider. You can't do it alone, so you must always invest in growing your network, just like you are always growing your skills.

    Here is something to keep in mind about your network that sounds counterintuitive. Your strong network ties are the people you know well—close friends and family who give you a sense of support, comfort, and belonging. They also tend to know the same people and information you know. But your weak ties are the people you don't know well and with whom you probably don't interact much.

But make no mistake. While weak ties are usually tapped only for a specific purpose, their power is anything but weak. These ties are crucial in connecting you to new relationships and networks. They are usually well positioned to help you connect to more plays because they extend your reach beyond your current circle and networks of those you already know. While strong ties can help support you, weak ties are your essential bridge to new information.

With your own playbook, you never wait for your employer's performance review to decide if you are on the right track. You need to start by knowing what kinds of skills, experiences, contacts, networks, mentorship, etc., you need to help you get to your big vision goal. Then ask yourself if there are key skills you need to develop that are missing from what you are doing right now. Are there key experiences in your company or outside it that would be helpful to have? Can you negotiate to get those experiences? Are you satisfied with your compensation for the value you bring?

You must always build choice control and cushion at every step, or you are not playing the game intelligently. Everything you do has to increase your choice, control, and cushion. This is different than just making decisions based on what is in front of you. You have to make decisions in ways that always open up choices for you and keep you sustainable. You have to hedge risk and make some bets on the future that allow you to be positioned for success no matter what.

BUSINESS OF YOU GAME

Now that we no longer have a social contract to rely on, we cannot just manage our careers. In these times of greater uncertainty, we've learned that we can have a large salary and still be vulnerable due to some unexpected event from which we can't recover. So, we can't just focus on growth; we also must build our life infrastructure to succeed and thrive sustainably. Therefore, we need to not only play the Future of Work game. We also need to play the Business of You game.

We've been taught to play the game as employees and as consumers. As employees, we relied on our ascension on the career ladder to help us access other life ladders and benefits, such as the health benefits ladder, the property purchase ladder, and the retirement benefits ladder.

> We've been taught as consumers that as our careers grow and we begin to earn a higher salary, the excess money in our pockets is disposable income. We as consumers therefore fall victim to "lifestyle creep" because we raise our standard of living to match our salary.

The problem is that this is one of the surest ways to lose the Business of You game—as our circumstances change, our lifestyle then must radically shift, and worse yet, there is no plan for emergencies or for the future.

SHIFT PARADIGM

Therefore, in order to not just play strong offense but also play strong life defense and rebound from setbacks, we must power our own economic engine as the Business of You, not just power the US economic engine as consumers. Our engine must be built not on what we spend but on our ability to create the safety and resilience we need today as well as the peace of mind that we need for the future.

Consider this: Companies don't just manage the products they sell. They must also manage the company itself in a way that allows it to grow regardless of which products they sell today. They must build it to last, not just to sell. So, just like a business CEO, you must manage your whole life, not just your talent, as a product to grow your income.

YOUR BLUEPRINT BUSINESS OF YOU GROWTH ENGINE™

To support your standard of living as well as your future development growth, your Blueprint Business of You Engine™ requires a few critical tanks that you need to fill to keep your economic engine running well:

- **The tank that powers your basic living security**
    1. Basic security: Through the strong offense of your Future of Work career strategy, you can build your basic living security to be able to afford the essentials to live.

- **The tanks that power your future development and ability to be resilient**
    2. Safety net security: Create safety-net emergency savings in case something goes wrong.

3. Risk security: Secure key insurance policies such as medical insurance, home insurance, car insurance, and life insurance to hedge against risk.

4. Savings and growth opportunity fund: Establish a fund that helps you save, grow, and plan for your future.

5. Wealth building and retirement security: Allow yourself to create wealth and position yourself for retirement with these vehicles.

 **LEVEL 4**

WINNING THE CHAMPIONSHIP BY MAKING PLAYS OVER MULTIPLE ROUNDS

Playing the game of life sustainably means that not only do we know how to navigate today to be successful; we also know how to be prepared for tomorrow. Thus, we can approach the future with peace of mind that we can not only absorb any unexpected shocks but are prepared for times of instability.

LIFE NAVIGATION GAME

Businesses future proof themselves by constantly being aware of the headwinds that can derail their plans and taking advantage of tailwinds that can provide an unexpected boost to growth.

They conduct regular SWOT (strengths, weaknesses, opportunities, threats) analyses to continually assess whether they are positioned for success, especially in uncertain times. That is why, in addition to your Blueprint Life and Business Model Canvas, you must regularly update your plays based on your SWOT analyses to navigate and build your own resilience against uncertainty.

Being future proofed brings you the peace of mind you seek, which comes from knowing the answers to the following questions:

- How strong is your career strategy?
- How well are you leveraging your strengths for greater power?
- How game intelligent are you?
- How diversified are your options?
- How well positioned are you to take advantage of greater opportunity?
- How strong is your economic engine, and how resilient does it allow you to be?
- How active are you in monitoring the changing winds?

TELLING YOUR STORY ACROSS MULTIPLE ROUNDS OF THE GAME OF LIFE

We are all familiar with a résumé. It is the most common way we tell the story of our job experiences to potential employers. Today, however, we need to see our career portfolio as just as important to tell our story to ourselves, even before we tell our story to others. One of the key lessons I teach in our Blueprint Life School is the importance of being able to tell your story in a way that extends beyond a résumé. That is because résumés are supposed to tell a story of a very linear career with no gaps, one that follows an extremely logical and sequential path.

FROM RÉSUMÉ TO CAREER PORTFOLIO

That kind of career is no longer the path we follow; therefore, a résumé is no longer sufficient for telling the story of careers today, which are more nonlinear. Portfolios include experiences and skills that aren't on a résumé, yet often future proof our careers. It includes our unique combination of skills, experiences, and talents that can be mixed, matched, and blended in different ways. It's about intentionally creating and curating a career that changes and evolves over time.

For example, what ties my story of working as a clinical psychologist, a leadership and performance consultant for large national Fortune 1000 companies, an executive and personal consultant, a chief officer of a foundation, and CEO of a nonprofit organization all together is that at the core, I desire to solve big challenges involving how to grow and lead, particularly through disruptive change.

You should build lifelong habits of growing your portfolio and telling your story. The more you figure out what you've learned from your experiences, what your transferrable skills are, and how to tell a compelling story of your unique advantage, the clearer you will be on where you're trying to go.

CHAPTER 9

BLUEPRINT 3

FROM LIFESPAN TO HEALTHSPAN

A sustainable human community is designed in such a manner that its ways of life, technologies, and social institutions honor, support, and cooperate with nature's inherent ability to sustain life.
—FRITJOF CAPRA

THE MASTERY BLUEPRINT

The way we used to play the game of life was that you studied hard for the first couple of decades so that you could work hard for the next several decades. You then were supposed to arrive at a place called success, happiness, and fulfillment from that hard work. You were then supposed to be able to retire securely for the remaining decades of your life.

We were reasonably assured that this path would work if we put in the hard work required. With continued effort, our standard of living and quality of life would lift, and we would not go backward because our education created a floor and insulator for us.

OUR FUTURE WAS TAKEN CARE OF FOR US

Life infrastructure and scaffolding were provided for us. From the previously clear education to career paths in stable industries to clear nine-to-five workdays that put boundaries between our work and life to the long-term stability with defined retirement benefits, we were able to work toward some basic level of stability and security and live a life with built-in infrastructure that helped us stay sustainable.

WE HAD A LESS CHALLENGING SHORT-TERM NAVIGATION CONTEXT

We did not live in a context of constant change and disruption. The load was not as cumulatively or collectively heavy for such a prolonged period of time.

In the old blueprint, we got safety, security, and sustainability built into the plan. It provided structure, stability, and momentum based on hard work, and increasing security with your increasing mastery. All of this meant that previously when we reached success, our security and sustainability used to come along for the ride because our lives were inextricably intertwined with the infrastructure and scaffolding that our employers built for us.

CONTEXT MATTERS

 ### THE GAME IS DIFFERENT

We managed our careers while our employer managed our benefits and life retirement. Now we must be able to do both, not simply manage our careers.

THE CONTEXT AND PACE OF CHANGE MAKE IT MORE DIFFICULT

The higher volatility that is a part of our backdrop brings a higher level of stress and exhaustion and is now a part of our lives. We are constantly under pressure and experiencing mental, economic, and physical fatigue. The constant high volatility of the world means that we need to play the game in tougher conditions.

WHAT THIS MEANS

Success is no longer a place of arrival. Basic life assumptions and rites of passage that we used to mark success no longer apply. Obtaining success is not the same as sustaining success, particularly in constant uncertainty. This means that knowing what it takes to succeed is not enough. We must learn how to be personally sustainable, not just successful, in order to maintain our well-being and build our resilience and sustainability in a more volatile world.

In my career, I've had the opportunity to work with people from all walks of life. Whether we are executives or entrepreneurs, new to our careers or in life transition, what we all have in common is that our lives are more complex than ever. Balancing our lives and careers, relationships, housework, and children means that our responsibilities and commitments are endless. Whether it's making to-do lists so we can stay on track or never really feeling that we can be present enough to enjoy any moment because we have to keep all the plates of our lives spinning, we are often exhausted by our lives.

So, even if we do everything right and attain a certain level of success, it does not mean we will stay there. We may now attain growth and success, but that is disconnected from our well-being, our quality, and our standard of living.

THE GAP

Chasing the dream is not the same as sustaining it. We now need to build sustainability into our navigation. Previous success markers were age-based lifespan markers of external success. Now, we need stage-based healthspan markers for sustainable success.

So, the American Dream is no longer just about current success. It is about our ability to generate personal and economic well-being today and in the future sustainably. We now have to learn a new game for living in our new context of uncertainty, change, and disruption.

SHIFT PARADIGM FROM THIS...

TO THIS:

THE INNOVATOR BLUEPRINT

HEALTHSPAN FOCUS

Financial success and lifetime security no longer go hand in hand. We must all now manage our well-being, quality, and standard of living for lifelong sustainability.

We have gone from thinking we arrive at success and security based on salary to also needing to manage our sustainability. We must increase our capacity by increasing our economic, mental, career, and lifestyle healthspan in addition to the known benefits of increasing our physical healthspan.

 NEW GOAL

Before, getting to career success was the main goal, and the rest was supposed to follow. Now, we need to also learn the skills to actively self-manage our lives, optimize our fulfillment and passions, and expand our lives more fully by increasing our healthspan, quality of life, and standard of life. We do so by knowing how to manage our well-being and by growing our strength, resilience, and endurance to play the game sustainably over multiple rounds.

THE BASICS

The new game of life is longer and requires that we have a different level of mental, financial, and economic conditioning; training fitness; and know-how to build the capacity to perform at a higher level in all the areas holistically in order to be sustainable and not suffer constant insecurity. We are living longer but not healthier. We need a new strategy for managing the increased economic and personal load and the toll exacted by our context that pulls us downward. We must value the importance of our underlying health, not just how we appear on the outside.

> The new game of life is longer and requires that we have a different level of mental, financial, and economic conditioning; training fitness; and know-how to build the capacity to perform at a higher level in all the areas holistically in order to be sustainable and not suffer constant insecurity.

Increasing your personal and economic well-being and healthspan means expanding your capacity to meet current and future personal and economic demands. Given that our context is one of greater friction, we need to be able to achieve our goals of success, happiness, and fulfillment while increasing our health by expanding our capacity to meet the increased friction and life demands. We must also build and maintain our standard and quality of living by building the needed economic, career, mental, and lifestyle scaffolding that we now need.

NO LONGER JUST GROWTH AT ALL COSTS

Success is no longer about a number that signals wealth; it is about underlying health, which is critical to development. We have gone from a place of arrival called "success" that was a number to now prioritizing the underlying health we can't see. It is about the growth of stages of underlying health, not the outward signs of success that are used to signal the arrival.

We need to train to sustain and build what is no longer there and to become more resilient and sustainable in the face of increased life pressure.

Given the accordion nature of our lives, we can no longer assume that success will be linear or will follow a straight-upward trajectory— or that it will be without contractions. Success is no longer a one-and-done, which means that we should not use salary or a static retirement savings number as a marker that we have arrived and that we can now coast through life.

Life is happening fast, and the pace of change is increasing. What gives the impression that we have arrived today might quickly leave us vulnerable tomorrow. We need to innovate to grow in change and disruption, and we need to consistently grow our healthspan so that we can be successful today, be prepared for tomorrow, and have peace of mind so that, regardless of what happens, we are able to meet those challenges. We need a different set of fundamentals to navigate this harsher climate.

THE POWER OF SUSTAINABILITY

We no longer just passively move through life based on our degrees, measuring growth by outside metrics like our salary. Sustainability is about growing our ability to be stronger within ourselves.

We must deliberately move from one stage to the next by learning to develop our underlying economic and personal health, well-being, and fitness. We must build our capacity to be resilient in the face of increasing demand. We must create peace of mind that, regardless of context, we can build the high quality of life and standard of life we seek.

NEW PARADIGM: HEALTHSPAN SUCCESS MARKERS

To gauge our sustainability, we don't just need to map our success to the old rites of passage that helped us gauge whether we were on track in life or falling backward in the old paradigm. It is no longer just about short-term growth; it is also about long-term viability and sustainability.

Now, we must gauge our healthspan, not only our lifespan, which indicates the strength of our life infrastructure, personal and economic health, and resilience and sustainability to manage our present and the future.

THE HEALTHSPAN ROAD MAP

STRESS ZONE

The pace of our lives has accelerated. We were used to a few key transitions and stress points throughout our lifetime. Now, there are many seismic shifts. This means that we feel increasingly fragmented and disjointed.

OUR NEW NORMAL

The friction is harsh and is creating a new normal: one where we are under constant threat. The threats include financial fears that loom large; life uncertainty weighs on us, as does the toll of personal and world trauma, not to mention workplace stress and information overload.

This means that even when you've arrived at your place of success today, you still may not be able to meet the future with confidence. So even if you are comfortable today, you are still worried and insecure about the future. Success, therefore, does not assure peace of mind about the future. Our environment of friction is now key. The constant friction you face is what is causing stress. You must, therefore, increase your ability to be sustainable in uncertainty and in an environment of constant friction.

A BODY ON HIGH ALERT

Stress and the resulting burnout has been called the "health epidemic of the 21st century." In our fast-paced VUCA world, this impacts our well-being and ability to function at high levels. This issue is so pervasive that by 2019, the World Health Organization classified burnout as an official diagnosis associated with increased rates of heart attacks, hypertension, and ulcers, as well as tension headaches and migraines. All stress isn't created equal, so first, let's discuss how stress impacts performance.

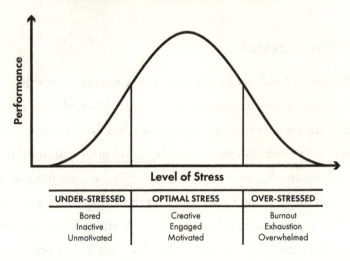

The curve suggests that performance increases with stress, but only up to a point. When stress levels are too low or too high, performance deteriorates.

The relationship between performance and stress is in the shape of an "inverted U" curve, meaning that elevated levels of stress up to a certain point help us before becoming detrimental. So when you are performing under a deadline, doing something new, or feeling energized and focused—especially if what you are doing matches your talents, passions, and interests—these all produce a stress response that will result in elevated physiological arousal, often associated with the release of cortisol, the main stress hormone. But here is the problem. Aside from the fast pace of the world, what is happening today is constant, disruptive change; therefore, our bodies are spending too much time in this extreme. It is moving us to fatigue, exhaustion, poor health, burnout, and breakdown.

So now, let's discuss what happens when we spend too much time on this extreme right end of the curve—constant high stress and burnout. When faced with threats, our body goes into a fight-flight-or-freeze response. Today's threats are the constant change and disruption of our world. When our bodies feel threatened, the primal, more emotional parts of our brains take over.

What distinguishes VUCA threats to our survival from smaller changes in our lives is the speed at which they happen. These disruptions are now more compressed. The change is also constantly happening in a way that is disorienting, creating big disruptions to our worldview, such as how we understand our work and life. We are wired for predictability and stability based on past experience. Now this constant uncertainty breeds a feeling of disempowerment and lack of control and agency.

THE BIOLOGY OF STRESS AND BURNOUT ... AND THE CONSEQUENCES

Your physiological responses are controlled by two systems: the parasympathetic and sympathetic nervous systems.

- Sympathetic for when you are in fight-or-flight
- Parasympathetic for when you are at rest

Rest, digest, and recover. In fact, the body is designed to spend most of its time at rest. The stress response is designed to go off only for a short time until you are out of harm's way. Ideally, we strive to have a balance between the two. Too much time in stress mode leads to burnout, because the stress response suppresses the immune system and tissue repair system, among others, to push blood to arms and legs to fight or run. Chronic stress mode keeps the immune system suppressed 24-7, which is why burnout comes with so many health risks. Chronic stress also strips your emotional resources until there is nothing left to counter the drain. It's a "gradual depletion over time of individuals' intrinsic energetic resources."

The result is a three-way mind-body shutdown—emotional exhaustion, physical fatigue, and cognitive weariness. Numbness and cynicism set in. You may feel a sense of depersonalization and a lack of accomplishment. Withdrawal, detachment from work and relationships, and symptoms of depression mark the advanced stages of the cycle. Cognitively, you lose sight of time because you live in the right now. You can't see the future. You are in protective mode and loss aversion because your focus is "How do I hold on?"

While burnout doesn't happen all at once, most people ignore the signals of burnout. The adaptive process of chronic stress thrives on this, because the adrenaline racing through your body to help you keep working harder masks the damage to overtaxed organs.

And even beyond burnout and its impact on our lives, stress has long been known to increase our vulnerability to addictions. While drugs and alcohol are some of the more common compulsive behaviors people might engage in, any kind of behaviors that provide some initial relief, such as turning to comfort foods, can also become addictive when coping with stress.

 **LEVEL 2**

NEW FOUNDATIONAL HEALTH, WELL-BEING, AND FITNESS FOR DAILY LIVING

To go from the tightrope of lifestyle stress in our lives to more sustainable daily living, in this second stage we will discuss the key goals of how to recover from too much life pressure and not enough bandwidth and how to restore the basic level of safety and security needed to function. We will also discuss how to build the foundational health, well-being, and fitness we need to have control over our day-to-day lives and to be able to meet our goals.

Our well-being is not just the absence of disease or illness. It's a combination of our physical, mental, emotional, economic, and social health factors. Our personal and economic well-being is strongly linked to happiness and satisfaction, as every aspect of our lives influences our well-being.

The first goal in building foundational health, well-being, and fitness for daily living is restoring our basic health vitals. When we go to the doctor, they check our vitals, such as our pulse, heart rate, blood pressure, etc. These vitals are basic and foundational to our functioning. Similarly, we need to get to a state of safety in our life vitals.

STEP 1: FUEL FOR RESTORING BASIC HEALTH

There is a burnout epidemic. Yet we are often told to just carry on. We are told how we can change our mindset or learn more productivity hacks. However, when someone is physically hurt—they break their ankle, for example—we all know that any attempt to play on a broken ankle will only make the problem worse. When someone is physically hurt, they cannot just carry on. Similarly, you cannot just dig deeper to be more productive while burning out. You must treat this the same way you would treat broken bones. You cannot play a game on a broken foot, nor can you continue to function when you are mentally depleted, because you are doing more harm. Here is what you should do instead.

Rest, Recovery, and Periodization

Sport sciences teach us the principle of rest and recovery, which suggests that rest and recovery from the stress of exercise must take place in proportionate amounts to avoid placing too much stress on the body. This systematic approach to rest and recovery has led exercise scientists and athletes to divide the fitness training phases into blocks or periods.

The principle of periodization suggests that training plans incorporate phases of stress followed by phases of rest. Without periodization, the stress from exercise would continue indefinitely, eventually leading to fatigue, possible injury, and overtraining. The energy spent balanced by the ability to recover and renew is key. The more energy you spend, the more you must recover. The rest and recovery principle is critical to achieving fitness gains. The body simply cannot tolerate too much stress and will, over time, "shut down" to protect itself.

Getting enough sleep is key to physical recovery. Exercise that raises your heart rate is effective for both mental and emotional recovery. Being out in nature, having time to quiet your mind, and connecting with friends and loved ones are also ways to renew your energy.

> While many people view this kind of downtime as not getting anything done, we should see downtime as *necessary* to get things done. Research has revealed that mental breaks increase productivity, replenish attention, solidify memories, and encourage creativity.

This is because when the brain is resting, it isn't unproductive. On the contrary, downtime improves the mental processes that allow us to live happier, more fulfilling, and less stressed lives. The default mode network (DMN) is the part of the brain that activates when we are not focused on any particular task. Giving our mind time to utilize the DMN is crucial to creatively solving problems. Think about how many times you have aha moments while you are in the shower. That is because this kind of unconscious mental activity is enabled when we have downtime. Downtime replenishes our attention, improves our motivation, and encourages productivity. It is also essential for high performance.

STEP 2: MANAGING YOUR LOAD

When our smartphones reach 20 percent battery charge, they allow us to turn on a power-saving mode that will reduce background activities, reduce screen timeout, and decrease screen brightness to stretch the battery life by avoiding actions that keep the screen on, maintain a constant internet connection, process too much information, and limit connectivity.

Similarly, when we are in survival mode, we have limited power and energy, both financially and emotionally. This means we are operating with a lowered bandwidth, so we need to move beyond our rest and recovery cycles and learn to actively manage our mental, financial, career-, and lifestyle-loads.

When you have reduced bandwidth, you do not have full use of your resources. What this feels like is that you have difficulty attending, as your life is pulling your brain in too many directions. You are dealing with too many upheavals. You have difficulty connecting things in a way that is executable. Everything takes too much brain capacity, so you have to realize that mentally, physically, emotionally, financially, and in your work, you're going to need to hyperfocus on getting yourself to a place where you have more capacity available to you.

Mental. Our mental capacity is finite. Think of it this way:

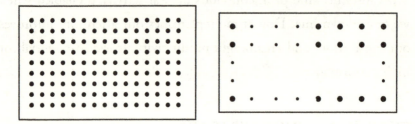

Fully available versus mentally depleted.

The first illustration represents our mental capacity when it is fully available. When we are under stress, living in survival mode or burnout mode, our mental real estate is not fully available, as represented in the second illustration. Therefore, we need to create strong hedges of protection to manage our mental load and reduce our stressors as we continue to regain our full mental capacity.

Financial. All the worrying about unpaid bills or loss of income can trigger anxiety symptoms such as a pounding heartbeat, sweating, shaking, or even panic attacks. A number of studies have demonstrated a relationship between financial worries and mental health problems such as depression, anxiety, and substance abuse. To manage the financial stress, we need to find ways to free up cash and stop the financial bleeding by creating a plan for tightening our budget.

Lifestyle. We live in a noisy world with many people and companies constantly competing for our attention in the attention economy. We must work to remove many of the constant distractions and interruptions that we have grown accustomed to in our lives.

Work. When our work intrudes after hours in the form of emails and other work alerts, it can cause spikes of stress that lead to adverse effects, including insomnia. Creating greater boundaries between our work and personal lives helps to create a stress buffer.

STEP 3: BUILDING YOUR FOUNDATIONAL HEALTH

The ABCs of foundational health. Just as we have recognized the importance of protecting the sustainability of our planet, the focus on personal sustainability is a parallel switch in our paradigm and life strategy to protect our own longevity through the things we may not see: our underlying health, fitness, and resilience in all areas of our life.

FIGURE 9.3: LIFESPAN VERSUS HEALTHSPAN

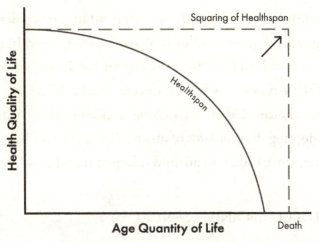

Your lifespan is the length of your life. Healthspan is the length of time you're healthy. Lifespan doesn't matter if you are not healthy enough to enjoy it. Building foundational health is how you "square the curve."

The key to sustainability is that you must grow and develop in a way that increases underlying health—in other words, growing healthspan as well, not just growing at all costs. It is paying attention to the things you may do that get a result but that make you weaker, more vulnerable, and unhealthier and shorten your overall healthspan and resilience. This also allows you to build the quality and standard of living that is important to you.

TWO KEY PARADIGM SHIFTS

Growing your healthspan, not just your lifespan, relies on new fundamentals and paradigm shifts in our habits so that we can build sustainably to increase our capacity and longevity for daily living and higher performance over time.

LIVING CONSCIOUSLY

We currently live unconsciously, spending our time on endless doomscrolling; adopting every influencer trend; letting algorithms decide what we see and read; relying only on Siri for directions. These are some of the ways we now live life unconsciously. We no longer make deliberate choices. Others are making decisions on our behalf, and we are adopting the standards of others. This is poor life hygiene, and the consequence is that we are now asleep at the wheel of our lives.

BUILDING CLEAN AND ESSENTIAL

We need to build our lives cleanly and essentially to be present and consciously choose what happens in our lives. This will interrupt the pattern of living based on a series of automatic responses by not attaching ourselves or our identity to anything but what we have deliberately chosen. We must increase the control of our life real estate by increasing our ability to think, create, and control our time, not just live in habit.

Living a low-quality, unconscious life prevents us from developing our own natural instincts. A low quality of life results in life disengagement, which is the consequence of living on autopilot even though we may be doing a lot of things. We end up being creatures of habit instead of having novel experiences, because we don't know what animates us and lights us up within. This is a near-life experience. We end up chasing life, not living it authentically, because the quality of our experiences does not fill us up.

Personal fulfillment occurs when your experience reflects your inner values rather than distracts you from them. That's what creates an animated, resonant, and sustainable life. Being personally fulfilled is being engaged with yourself, because you are living inside out. Living connects you back to what is true about you inside. It brings you to your peak desire, and it is sustainable because it is internally driven.

RETURNING TO YOUR CORE

Building a clean and essential lifestyle means going back to the basics of how we interact with the world around us. Our daily lives used to have natural ways that allowed us to stay present and allowed us to connect our brain, body, and emotions naturally without the intrusion of external aids making those decisions for us. While technological progress is good, we also used to learn to write in full paragraphs, so we naturally learned how to develop our thoughts fully. We interacted directly and face to face with others individually, which allowed us to slow down and determine what we really thought instead of only exposing ourselves to what was trending. We were able to separate the thoughts of others from our own thoughts. These were all ways of developing personal intelligence, the basic building block of living a clean and essential lifestyle.

Similarly, building a clean and essential financial lifestyle requires that you untie your decisions on how you spend your money from the weight of external expectations, validation, status signaling, or anything that can otherwise control you. To separate your needs and loves from wants and likes, you must learn to be sensitive to the functional benefit of your purchases rather than how the things you purchase make you feel. You need to be aware of the psychology of spending and the cognitive biases that can lead you to make suboptimal financial decisions. Learning these innate biases that have tripped you up in the past can help you make better financial decisions in the present and future.

CLEAN AND ESSENTIAL LIVING

Here is a checklist to help you determine whether you are living clean and essentially or having a low-quality life experience:

- Do you feel disengaged from your own life?
- Are your peak life experiences based on consuming something?
- Do you evaluate yourself mainly based on social comparison?
- Who controls your source of gratification? Is it you, or someone or something else?
- Who controls your fate? Is it you, or can something or someone else take it all away?

LIVING ORGANICALLY

We have removed the ways we used to be active naturally in our lives, the ways we used to build natural social connections in our lives, the psychological proximity we used to feel in real face-to-face relationships, the time spent outdoors and in nature, and the time we spent creating a rich inner life through play, reading, and music. It has been crowded out by the noisy, always-on, high friction of our daily and virtual lives.

We are now living outside-in instead of inside-out. What this typically looks like is that we are constantly relying on overproduced, big life moments in the hope that these will translate to our feeling something inside us. We lack the natural, organic daily and regular small moments that emanate and are amplified by what is inside us; instead, we rely on the artificially produced big moments that make it seem we are living a big life.

This outside-in living just leaves us feeling numb within. For many, this numbness can lead to some form of addiction, whether it is work, alcohol, gambling, social media, drugs, or spending. These addictions are not only unhealthy; they leave us even less available to ourselves and others.

So, the quality of our life must move from this outside-in experience to one built to organically and sustainably experience life. In the past, we were able to get much of what we needed to build our lives organically and sustainably through our natural life experiences. Now, our lifestyle is damaging our health. Therefore, we need a lifestyle that rebuilds what we need for health, well-being, and fitness naturally.

WHAT IS GROWING ORGANICALLY?

Growing organically is about natural and sustainable growth based on building sustainable lifestyle habits. As opposed to relying on the external and artificial environment around us, these green habits rely on our own neuroscience; our natural strengths; and building our mind, body, and emotional connections. So, we need to go back to the basics and (re)consider all the things that we need to build back into our lifestyle that we use to do more naturally.

THE GREEN AND ORGANIC LIFESTYLE NATURAL FOODS WE NEED

Our strengths and purpose as natural food. One reason we may be disengaged at work and not energized or thriving is that we are not using our strengths—what we are naturally good at—and we are not connected to our sense of purpose. Learning about yourself and what matters to you, your natural strengths, talents and gifts, is foundational for connecting and engaging in your life.

Connection as natural food. Humans are hardwired for connection. Neuroscience suggests that our brains are wired to connect with others; mirror neurons in our brains are stimulated when we're interacting with other people. Literally, when you are talking to someone, pathways in your brain light up to mirror the emotions and behaviors that this other person is conveying.

We also tend to believe that social and physical pain are radically different. Yet neuroscience suggests that the way our brains respond to them suggests they are "more similar than we imagine."

Our brains evolved to experience threats to our social connections in much the same way they experience physical pain. By activating the same neural circuitry that causes us to feel physical pain, our experience of social pain helps ensure the survival of our children by keeping them close to their parents. The neural link between social and physical pain also ensures that staying socially connected to others will be a lifelong need, like food and warmth.

Therefore, we need to view building real social connections as a basic need. The Centers for Disease Control and Prevention suggests dedicating time and attention to developing and maintaining relationships by focusing on building high-quality, strong, and meaningful social connections.

Lifestyle as natural food. One consequence of our highly digitally connected world is the increase in the time we all spend in front of screens. This high screen time, however, may come at the expense of the green time that we need for our well-being. Spending time in nature can help improve your mood and reduce feelings of stress. Studies have shown that our minds and bodies relax in a natural setting. This increases feelings of pleasure and can help us concentrate and focus more effectively, according to studies in the National Library of Medicine.

When we think of movement, we often associate it with high-intensity workouts. However, movement takes many forms, and many types of movement are beneficial for our bodies and minds. Regularly moving our body helps relieve stress, helps emotions move through our bodies, and strengthens our connection with our bodies.

> **The natural nutrition we need.** Just like what we put into our physical body is the basis of our physical health, our mental diet is the basis of our personal well-being. When you feel good, your brain naturally releases happiness chemicals or hormones. We can strengthen our neural connections and naturally increase our happiness by getting our daily DOSE of four main brain chemicals: dopamine, oxytocin, serotonin, and endorphins.

- Dopamine: Known as the "feel-good" hormone, dopamine is a neurotransmitter that's an important part of your brain's reward system. It's associated with pleasurable sensations, along with learning, memory, and more. Exercise, listening to music, and meditation naturally increase dopamine.

   Beware of too much!
  The effects of dopamine are fleeting due to its instant gratification feeling, which leaves you desiring more. The overstimulation of dopamine can become a real problem because of its addictive nature. It is closely tied to developing bad habits or addictions.

- Oxytocin: Often called the "love hormone," oxytocin is essential for childbirth, breastfeeding, and strong parent-child bonding. It can also help promote trust, empathy, and bonding in relationships. Hugging, spending time with loved ones, and cuddling with your pet are some of the ways to naturally increase oxytocin.
- Serotonin: This hormone and neurotransmitter helps regulate your mood as well as your sleep, appetite, digestion, learning ability, and memory. Working out, sun exposure, and meditation are all good ways to naturally increase serotonin levels.
- Endorphins: These hormones are your body's natural pain relievers, which it produces in response to stress or discomfort. You can naturally increase your endorphin levels when you engage in reward-producing activities such as eating, laughing, working out, dancing, or having sex.

BLUEPRINT 3: FROM LIFESPAN TO HEALTHSPAN

 **LEVEL 3**

CONDITIONING FOR HIGH PERFORMANCE

Level 2 was about building a clean, organic, healthy foundation and growing more consciously with natural fundamentals for daily living. This level lifts from the fundamentals to address how we can build the dynamism required for higher performance, especially under more pressure.

Our goal is to be economically, mentally, career, and life-strong, which means we need to expand our capacity to meet the increasing demands of performing under pressure. We need to develop the capacity and the instincts that allow us to play and thrive in these environments and to be resilient in the face of unforeseen setbacks so that we can make life choices, build assets, and absorb financial shocks.

We therefore need to build greater capacity to manage the greater demands of this long game.

So, like athletes and CEOs, we must know how to manage this life game in multiple rounds since, as we've established, it is not one-and-done. This means learning how to be resilient so we can rebound, play the long game, and keep our goals in mind.

Resilience is the ability to function effectively and sustainably, even under the most difficult circumstances. It is about how well you can weather the storm and come back. Resilience is critical for playing the game sustainably.

OUR LANGUAGE LIMITS OUR UNDERSTANDING

Now that we are living in a time of greater stress and uncertainty, one big challenge is that our current language limits our understanding of how to lift from the building blocks of foundational health to building personal and economic strength, fitness, and resilience.

The Language of Mental Health

Mental health had long been regarded as a taboo topic and was often equated only with mental illness. So, the social shift to acknowledging the importance of taking care of our mental health over the last few years has been a really good thing, as it brought conversations about mental health out of the shadows.

We've only just begun discussing mental well-being and how to protect our mental wellness or recover when we feel we have lost our center of gravity. We do not really discuss or learn about how to build the higher performance we all now need. Usually, the language of mental strength and resilience is reserved for athletes, but we all now must perform like athletes mentally to meet the demands of today. So, we either understand mental illness on one end or high mental strength and resilience on the other end, but nothing in between that will allow us to live sustainably.

The Language of Financial Health

For most people, not only was money a taboo topic, but they measured their financial strength largely on the size of their one annual salary. Six figures meant you could rest easy because you were strong and would be resilient.

Many grew up not talking about finances in their family because their parents did not feel comfortable discussing it. As kids, they therefore believed it was okay not to learn how to manage their finances. Even discussing salaries was considered taboo. That barrier has recently been broken, however, as employees have begun sharing their salaries on social media for greater transparency and equity.

We've learned that our credit scores are a good way to assess our financial health. We often only deliberately create a budget when we are in a financial pinch or in trouble. On the other end of the financial spectrum, learning how to build wealth and invest seems to apply only to a much smaller percentage, but we all now must learn how to manage our economic well-being like a CEO to meet today's demands.

So we either understand credit cards and basic budgeting on one end or wealth building and investing on the other, but not too much else in between that will allow us to live sustainably.

RESILIENCE: JUST BEYOND YOUR COMFORT

Building resilience requires that we challenge ourselves mentally, professionally, and financially to persist despite discomfort and uncertainty. We need to build resilience by moving from the fitness mode of the previous level to the challenge mode of this level.

Challenge mode means that you are proactively challenging yourself to expand your comfort zone. This expansion allows you to bring the unfamiliar into the familiar. It is where you move from familiar responses to a more strategic, innovative, big-picture response to the novel situations we keep facing.

In this challenge mode, you have to learn to perform in new contexts because constant change and disruption—and therefore unpredicted and unplanned circumstances—have become the norm. When we have a resilient lifestyle, we are nimble, dynamic, and agile. Professionally, we have more than one stream of income, which allows us to make a number of diversified plays through our career strategy, and game intelligence, which allows us to make many plays. Mentally, we can bounce back from setbacks and bounce forward while we manage our emotions. Financially, we are literate and have a safety net as well as growth engines for the future.

Mental Resilience

Muscles grow stronger only when we keep adding resistance, yet we consider failure a bad thing even though it is simply a way to build natural resilience. Feedback allows us to get stronger when things don't go our way. Mental training is needed not just for learning the rules of the game itself but for the strength and resilience to keep playing when the outcome is uncertain; we need the endurance to play many rounds or to persevere when the last round has not gone our way.

Mastering the Mental Game

Most athletes would say that, at high levels of performance, the game is won or lost based on what you don't see: the Mental game. To master the Mental game, your instinct needs to be to look inside yourself for the next move, not outside yourself. Some people lose the belief that they can influence their own outcomes through their behavior. Rebounding is about how to regain your grasp of the world, of your game. It is not simply a set of actions on the outside; it is about what needs to be present inside you and what to do inside you. It requires you to bet on yourself and never quit on yourself.

You must learn to manage your emotions to build the resilience required to win a championship, not just a game. That is because when our emotions are high, our logic is low. When we allow ourselves to move into the more instinctive fight-flight-or-freeze mode, that kind of automatic response prevents us from accessing the full range of thinking we will need to be resilient. Especially under pressure, we need to be able to see things clearly.

Explanatory Style

A key to how we manage our emotions is our explanatory style. Psychologists use the term "explanatory style" to describe how people explain the events of their lives. When something happens, our explanatory style is part of how we process it, attach meaning to it, and assess it as a threat or a challenge. It's part self-talk and part self-perception, and it affects stress levels in multiple ways. Your explanatory style affects your life in ways you may not realize. It can also motivate you when you're faced with challenges or leave you feeling vulnerable to them.

These are the three parameters of explanatory styles:

1. Stable versus unstable: This has to do with how you perceive the permanence of a situation. Is it changing across time or unchanging? Do you expect things to get better or worse or stay exactly as they are for a long time?

2. Global versus local: Is a stressor universal throughout your life—is it pervasive, or is it specific to a part of your life?

3. Internal versus external: Do you see the cause of an event as within yourself—personalization—or outside yourself?

If you have a pessimistic explanatory style, meaning that you attribute negative events to internal, stable, and global causes, you are more likely to experience lower levels of motivation and to be less resilient.

Your explanatory style also matters because it is the hinge, the leverage, that allows you to see beyond what is happening at that moment. It allows you to look ahead and rely on higher coping skills to rebound and bounce forward to create the future.

Your internal leverage must allow you to be a HERO. This means that your explanatory style must allow you to create a sense of *hope* toward your goals. It allows you to have *efficacy*, a belief in your ability to produce a positive result. It allows you to be *resilient*, which is a positive way to cope even when you don't immediately see the next solution. It also allows you to have *optimism* so that you can remain positive about the likelihood of personal success.

Financial Resilience

To build financial strength, resilience, and endurance, you need financial leverage so that your money starts working for you. This is why it is important to build upon your Blueprint Business of You Engine™ for growth and now also create leverage.

There are different philosophies on how to think about our financial life, some of which have developed in response to the more uncertain times we face. Programs range from YOLO (you only live once), which philosophically encourages people to live for today since tomorrow seems so uncertain, on one extreme to savings and investment movements on the other extreme, which is all about saving everything today so that you can retire early.

Given that people are really looking to live a more integrated lifestyle of health, wealth, and happiness, neither extreme is aligned with the more holistic view of success. People, therefore, need new guidance to help them be resilient in uncertainty while still living and enjoying life in the present.

Our Blueprint Business of You Economic Engine™ is a paradigm-shifting system that combines our essentialism lifestyle approach with a financial system that helps you build the financial capacity and resilience to achieve the high-margin, high-cushion, high-quality life you desire while creating the high-leverage and high-growth economic engine needed to be sustainable.

LEVEL 4

PICTURES OF HEALTH

You would not operate a car without ever looking at the key indicators on the dashboard that let you know if it is safe to drive. You also know that you need to do more than just put gas in the car to keep it well maintained and extend the life of your car. Yet we do the opposite in our own lives than what we do to maintain our cars. Through our lifestyles, we drive ourselves mentally into the ground, and we spend ourselves into the ground without a good picture of our lifestyle or spending habits. Living without these key pictures of health only leads us to weaken ourselves in the short run and not build the right level of strength and resilience in the long run. As a result, we are shortening our healthspan.

ECONOMIC LIFE PICTURE

Critical financial pictures such as balance sheets, income statements, and cash flow statements will help you build your foundational health and create financial leverage through your Blueprint Business of You Economic Engine™. These three statements are necessary for anyone looking to manage their Business of You to provide a good picture of their financial health and strength.

THE NEW LIFE BLUEPRINT

PERSONAL LIFE PICTURE

One of the most common types of clients I work with is those who have what I call life stress and strain that they can't name. Here is what I mean by that. We've all heard stories of people who know something is medically wrong, but for whatever reason, the doctors are not able to provide a diagnosis. When they finally get a diagnosis, one of the things they talk about is the relief of finally being able to name what is wrong, the relief of being able to confirm that it is real, not all in their head, and that other people have had the same condition, so they are not alone.

> One of the most common types of clients I work with is those who have what I call life stress and strain that they can't name.

Similarly, many of my clients say they did everything right, but they still don't have peace of mind. They can't name, diagnose, or figure out what the problem is, so they don't know how to solve it. Once they understand the difference between their outward markers of success and foundational health and sustainability, they are in a much better position to do what they need to achieve the elusive peace of mind they seek.

When considering your own picture of well-being, a good way to do so is through a modified PERMA model. The model is modified to include what we all now look for in response to our constantly changing world—peace of mind.

Modified PERMA model of well-being:

- **P:** Peace of mind frees you of the anxiety and strain of a constantly changing or uncertain environment so you can thrive.
- **P:** Positive emotions fuel you on a day-to-day basis and help you feel good.
- **E:** You are engaged in your life; time stands still, you have moments of flow, and you are living at your highest.
- **R:** Your relationships are authentic connections.
- **M:** You have a sense of meaning and a purposeful existence.
- **A:** You have a sense of accomplishment in your life.

FOUR-QUADRANT LIFESTYLE

Usually when we are thinking about ways to assess and grow the different areas of our life, we approach our life assessment in a piecemeal fashion. For example, we approach our career growth separate from our financial growth, which is separated from our mental and lifestyle growth. We try to view and solve these one at a time. But our financial well-being is not separate from our career and economic engine, which are not separate from our mental and lifestyle well-being. These are all intertwined, and so we need to look at our lives in a more holistic way than what we are used to developing.

To get to the redefined success that we now want, we need to switch our paradigm to simultaneously pursuing the health, wealth, and happiness that we are looking for. Our Blueprint Four Quadrant Lifestyle Map™ can help you create the lifestyle that enables the integration of your doing and being—a lifestyle that enables you to thrive and bring your full self to each day. In other words, when considering what you do, your lifestyle should encourage your overall career, financial, life, mental, and physical well-being and fitness.

CHAPTER 10

BLUEPRINT 4

FROM CONSUMER MINDSET TO BUSINESS OF YOU MINDSET

Make sure your worst enemy doesn't live between your own two ears.
—LAIRD HAMILTON

THE MASTERY BLUEPRINT

Our old blueprint taught us how to acquire information and follow the rules. Our success was judged by how well we mastered the known. In the Mastery Blueprint, we were students who passively learned the information teachers dispensed. The exchange was generally one way. Your employer encouraged you to see your job as a family, where they took charge of your career and took care of you for life.

THE NEW LIFE BLUEPRINT

WHAT WE LEARNED

As consumers, businesses marketed to you to influence what you buy. From student to employee to consumer, our mindset was passive, whether we were relying on others to sell us the dream or on others to manage our dream and our future on our behalf.

DO-IT-YOURSELF CONTEXT

We no longer live in that stable, predictable world. Constant change and uncertainty now require active life management. We can no longer just manage our careers. We need to manage our more challenging present day, our ability to be resilient in case of setbacks, our future, and our retirement. We no longer live in an industrial economy that rewards what we have mastered. We must now be innovators of our future, not masters of the past and present.

BLUEPRINT 4: FROM CONSUMER MINDSET TO BUSINESS OF YOU MINDSET

The problem is that the mastery mindset is no longer the mindset we need to manage ourselves and grow more innovatively in our new context. Yet we still see ourselves in a more passive way, and our habits are more passive.

SHIFT PARADIGM FROM THIS...

TO THIS:

THE INNOVATOR BLUEPRINT

BUSINESS OF YOU MINDSET

We need to go from our 20th century mastery mindset to a 21st century innovator mindset.

 NEW GOAL

We must be fully conscious and aware of the choices to lead and manage our lives, especially in uncertainty. Rather than having others take charge of our lives on our behalf and then being led to spend as consumers, we must stay in full control and fully manage what we can so that we can thrive in uncertainty.

 THE BASICS

TAKE-FULL-CHARGE MINDSET AND APPROACH

Constant change and uncertainty now require active life management, so we must have a take-full-charge mindset and approach. We need to not simply turn over control of our lives to others; we need to adopt a take-full-control mindset. By adopting a no-waiting, no-permission-required attitude toward business and life, we can create our own security and safety nets and reimagine how we shape our lives to achieve the inward and outward success we are looking for.

CONSTANT INNOVATION

We no longer live in an industrial economy that rewards what we have mastered. We must now be innovators of our future, not masters of the past and present. The mantra of innovate or die that applied to businesses also applies to how we must view our mandate in constant change and disruption.

THE BUSINESS OF YOU ROAD MAP

THE CONSUMER MINDSET

We live our lives based on consumer habits, mindsets, and viewpoints. As consumers, we look to marketers, advertisers, and influencers to subconsciously direct us to what we want. We rely on banks to tell us how much house we can afford. We follow people, experts, and trends to help us feel comfortable when we are on trend and to make decisions on our behalf. Then, at the start of each year, we create yearly vision statements and make resolutions we all know we will break by month three. We seek change in our lives as an exception instead of a strategy for continual growth.

But there is a cost to living based on these consumer habits. We no longer make conscious choices. We, as consumers, do not intentionally manage our lives. The consumer viewpoint is a consumer-center-of-gravity mindset. We do not lead or manage ourselves. Someone else provides the solutions and answers to fix it. We do not use tools for deliberate growth other than resolutions and vision statements. We are vulnerable because our psychology and cognitive biases as consumers are used against us.

Businesses do not survive if they simply consume their way through life, but we are expected to. Businesses rely on data, trends, forecasts, and insights to help them run and continually grow, especially in uncertainty. When they grow and innovate, they do not look to others to give them the "answer"; they look for the strategies and insights they can apply to help them make the best decisions on their own behalf.

Similarly, we need more than the yearly vision boards and resolutions we make at the start of the year, only to abandon them and allow everyone else to influence our direction for the rest of the year. We need to change the center of gravity from adopting the priorities of others who influence us to a mindset and identity that creates our own center of gravity and ecosystem, which increases our odds of success. The new mindset must be to get information that helps us grow and make better decisions and innovate, not just make better decisions on how to spend. We must also grow our ability to innovate as a habit instead of spending as a habit. We must now see ourselves as a growing business where we are fully in charge of leading and managing our lives, growth, and dreams through change and disruption.

 **LEVEL 2**

THE BUSINESS OF YOU MINDSET

We can no longer just manage our careers. We need to manage our more challenging present day, our ability to be resilient in case of setbacks, our future, and our retirement. So, we now must adopt a mindset that helps us manage ourselves with the same intentionality as a business start-up that must grow sustainably across our lifetime—the Business of You.

The mindset shift is from "work hard and wait for someone to notice you or decide for you" to "show up for yourself, decide for yourself, and achieve what you desire." You don't need anyone to choose you, appoint you, qualify you, or otherwise deem you worthy. You can speak on your own behalf. You must be your own translator of value and make your own decisions. You must have a bias for action and innovation in change and disruption. It is about self-leadership of yourself and of your life.

Our mindset can no longer be passive. We must be conscious and intentional to manage, protect, grow, and innovate. To do so, we must condition a new consciousness that will allow us to think without the biases that lead us. This requires self-leadership based on a Business of You–centered—not consumer-centered—identity.

Your identity, your essential you, is your center of gravity. It is your inner compass that guides you. It is your foundational core identity and knowledge of self.

Here are the three critical relationships we all must have with ourselves in the essential you—your *I Am*:

- **SELF-POSSESSION (A SENSE OF WHOLENESS)**

    To be self-possessed is to be calm, confident, and in control of your emotions. It's being able to have a heightened sense of awareness to know when and how you should care for yourself.

    This is in contrast to what we are told selflessness is—having no concern for self. Although helping others can benefit our health, happiness, and relationships, being too caring can sometimes have downsides. For example, selfless people may feel exploited in their interpersonal relationships or burned out in their jobs.

- **SELF-DETERMINATION (CONTRIBUTES TO YOUR MINDSET)**

    Self-determination is an idea that includes people choosing and setting their own goals, being involved in making life decisions, self-advocating, and working to reach their goals. Self-determination is less about control than about taking action in your life to get the things you want and need.

- **SELF-REALIZATION (MOVING TOWARD YOUR TRUE NORTH)**

    This is the "fulfillment by oneself of the possibilities of one's character or personality." It is the process of becoming aware of and understanding your true self through increased self-awareness and understanding. Essentially, your identity is the story you tell. What do you say to yourself about yourself? Are you able to hear the sound of your own voice? Can you see yourself? What is the story you tell yourself about yourself? Identity is the anchor within you.

Identity can be rooted in a couple different ways:

- **CONSUMER MINDSET**

    In service of a need inside. Your titles, your acquisitions, are how you get your self-esteem. They are how you feel worthy inside, and how you feel, see, and know who you are. You feel significant only in relation to something or someone else.

- **BUSINESS OF YOU MINDSET**

    In service of something greater than yourself, rooted in values and principles that are not feeding you but something more. You exist separate from these things. You get fed in other ways. This is the definition of self-assurance, as your self-assessment is independent of anyone or anything.

To get to the Business of You mindset, we need a strong center of gravity or a strong core identity to navigate life and stay on course, especially in uncertainty and times of change that challenge who we believe we are.

Yet most of us are consumer (other) centered, not Business of You (self) centered. We center our job titles and what we acquire as a stand-in for who we are. Your job title is not part of your *I Am*. These are things you do. This lack of core identity leaves us vulnerable, and we do not even realize it. If you are defined based on something that someone else can either give to you or take away from you, then someone else will always have the power to define you. When this happens, there will eventually be a disconnection from yourself, a complete disengagement from any real core of your own values.

For a strong core identity, we must get out of the habit of defining ourselves by things like our job titles. In other words, we must see ourselves as "I am a person who ..." versus "I am (the title itself)."

Self-leadership means you can't wait for someone to define you or your value, direction, or worth. Your foundation and core must be solid.

For a strong and independent sense of identity, or *I Am*, the power to define must stay with you. Your highest value must be free of anything that could put a lien on it or release toxic pollutants to your sense of *I Am*. Clean *I Am* living means that your *I Am* gives off no toxins. Your identity is attached only to you.

> **Here are ways to know if you have a foundationally clean *I Am* identity:**
>
> The sound of your voice must be independent from anything you do or that anyone says, either positive or negative.
>
> In uncertainty, the feedback for yourself must be independent from your environment. You must be able to locate yourself and find your way back home. It is the ability to see the truth of who you are. Can you value yourself without external validation and affirmation? When everything around you all goes away, are you still present?
>
> Are you able to locate yourself separate from external things and value yourself? Can you hear the sound of your own voice?

BLUEPRINT 4: FROM CONSUMER MINDSET TO BUSINESS OF YOU MINDSET

> When you take it all away, and when you can't hide, do you still know who you are?
>
> Is the source of your validation internal versus external? Are you defined by your circumstances, by other people, or by you?

 **LEVEL 3**

INNOVATION FOR CONTINUOUS CHANGE

Some athletes are known as great players based on how they play the game as we all understand it. Then there are others who are great not simply because they play the game exceptionally as we understand it but because they have created new ways to play the game that were previously unheard of. They leverage current talent with vision and creativity to change the game as we know it.

Stephen Curry fundamentally changed the game of basketball by focusing on his three-point shot long before it was acceptable to do so in the NBA. Now, based on his exceptional three-point shooting skills, he has inspired teams and players to embrace three-point shots.

Those who will survive today's economic environment and succeed in tomorrow's are those willing to reinvent themselves continually. So, you must define yourself not based on what you know today but on what you can know, what you can learn, what problems you must solve, and what value you can create to remain relevant. We must all innovate in response to our changing context, no matter where we are on our journey, if we are not just to survive but continue to grow and thrive despite change and disruption.

DYNAMISM AND INNOVATION

Innovation is the development of new ideas or the improvement of existing ideas. Innovators recognize when there's a need for improvement, and they use creativity to come up with ways to meet those needs.

Innovation helps businesses grow even in more difficult and uncertain times, and similarly, innovation is required for individuals to change and grow continuously. But innovation involves uncertainty, creativity, and a mindset that not all people have or are willing to embrace.

Companies usually focus on the external process of innovation, such as creating a consistent brainstorming process or reducing ambiguity. Yet people fail to innovate, not because they lack knowledge of an external process. They fail because they lack an internal process or the mindset required for innovation.

Being responsive to our environment is a mindset. We must develop a mindset that allows us to be more dynamic, agile, flexible, and resilient in uncertainty, which means that we need to center being dynamic, not just being degreed. Innovation requires a mindset of change agility—constantly anticipating, adapting, and finding opportunity in change.

WHAT IS CHANGE AGILITY?

An important predictor of success is the ability to grow, learn, adapt, change, and innovate to make things happen. The skills and mindsets required to rise in good, steady-state times are not the same as those needed to keep you moving forward in more volatile and uncertain times. Change agility is how we grow and adapt by creating solutions where none exist that help us sustain success regardless of the context.

You have to be able to change your moves in response to the context. Change agility can help us become future proofed. It fosters the ability to deal effectively with challenges and use them to our advantage to navigate change. Leverage is key, as change agility allows you to leverage change and disruption to accelerate your success: to not just adapt to change but to grow and innovate despite change.

THE ANATOMY OF INNOVATION

Personal innovation has three main internal processes:

1. An inner compass that grounds you in your foundational *I Am*
2. Your change agility that serves as the critical hinge between your *I Am* and your *I Can*
3. New *I Can* solutions that allow you to create the future innovatively

1. Your Inner Compass and the Paradox of Change

The paradox of change is that, even as we seek change and innovation, we must maintain a "changeless core." Your changeless core is your center of gravity—your strong core identity or *I Am* based on your sense of self-possession, self-determination, and self-realization.

The key is that your changeless core must be the anchor and security that exists inside you. Security no longer comes from outside us, as we have seen, so we must find it within and create our own security. When a person thinks about change, the primary element that makes them willing to take the risks that change and innovation require is the sense of security that comes from the changeless part of themselves. So those with an unshakeable core identity and enduring values are the ones most able to innovate sustainably.

Your changeless core is the inner security that assures you that you will not change or disappear and that you are not defined by any outcome or circumstance. In uncertainty, the feedback for yourself must be independent of your environment. You must be able to locate yourself and find your way back home. Your changeless core is also what allows you to see opportunity. It allows you to see the future regardless of what today looks like. It allows you to be future oriented instead of always looking in the rearview mirror. Your changeless core is what allows you to have a will that is enlarging you independent of your circumstance versus shrinking you under the weight of what you are managing in your present moment.

This strong core allows you to see yourself as constantly on a beginner's journey of innovation, reaching without ego and baggage to new visions of what is possible without stories that no longer serve you.

2. Change Agility

Your ability to maintain a core identity that can bend, not break, is foundational, as it is this identity that will determine what your risk tolerance is, how you respond to failure, and how you assess gains versus losses.

Detached exploration. Your relationship to failure is important. It matters whether you see failure as feedback about you or feedback about the situation.

When failure is seen only as feedback about a situation, it allows for unattached exploration. If your identity is wrapped up in an outcome, it also means you will be strongly attached to some ideas and, conversely, less open to letting go of some ideas and trying new ones. Those who are more prone to detached exploration, the basis of innovation, are able to postpone fixation on an idea and stay open to exploring and diverging from different ideas and possible directions before converging and deciding on any specific ideas.

Dynamism and dexterity. Mental dynamism, dexterity, and nimbleness foster a mindset that allows you to be dynamic. You constantly deconstruct and reconstruct ideas and situations in response to your context, taking advantage of opportunities and avoiding challenges. Dynamism and dexterity help you expose yourself to more ideas, open yourself up to more choices and options, and be responsive to the world around you.

3. New Solutions

Pivoting to new solutions is about finding ways to create and innovate that lift from our center of gravity. To do so, we need to see a new, compelling vision that inspires us based on what we want, our set of deeper values and vision for ourselves. We can then choose new solutions that lift from our strengths and mission in work and life.

THE PARADOX OF EXPERIENCE

Innovation requires that we constantly see ourselves on a beginner's journey. This journey is often short-circuited by the paradox of experience. For people who are considered experts or consider themselves very experienced in their fields, their professional identities are based on the accumulation of knowledge and expertise. It is how they are rewarded.

However, the most courageous part of the beginner's journey is the courage that comes from a willingness to not define yourself by what you know but by what you *can* know. It is about changing your mindset from being judged on the one mountain you have successfully climbed to knowing that you will have a few acts across your lifetime.

True innovators must have an identity supported by this pursuit and not need the constant affirmation of past successes or the present affirmation of titles, etc., to reinforce their own worth and journey.

The paradox is that "experience" is a double-edged sword. What you know is not the same as what you can create. You must be willing to fight the fear of wondering whether or not you have a second or third act in you. You do.

THE UNDISCIPLINED PURSUIT OF MORE

Another way we short-circuit innovation is by the undisciplined pursuit of more. Innovation is about lifting from a core center of gravity, lifting from strength, and shifting or pivoting into new areas of potential strength.

Sometimes we see people and companies drift into areas that are usually only about following the money. It is a "hot" opportunity, everyone is doing it, and it looks like easy money with quick returns. When these discontinuous moves are very inconsistent with any core values, core strengths, or larger vision we have set for ourselves or our business, we often see strong, quick growth followed by the eventual crash and burn, because this type of undisciplined growth is often unsustainable in the long run.

 **LEVEL 4**

FROM THE SINGULAR JOURNEY TO SUCCESS MINDSET TO THE BUSINESS OF YOU ECOSYSTEM MINDSET

In the old paradigm of how we develop, growth was a one-and-done singular journey to success. We assumed that once we got on our career path, we would be set for life. If you felt like you needed a new path, that was an exception. We were supposed to keep climbing the ladder successfully, and we would, if needed, turn to personal or professional development and coaching to help us get back on our path or create new paths. These were considered exceptions to the journey and not an integral part of our singular journey upward. But businesses do not see it this way. They put themselves in networks and equip themselves with the tools, resources, and information to make better decisions.

WHY START-UPS NEED ECOSYSTEMS TO SURVIVE AND THRIVE

In the wake of constant disruptions, it is not easy for start-ups to survive all the factors in their environment that can have a detrimental impact on their survival and growth. Ecosystems that provide entrepreneurs support in the form of human capital, education, training, and financial support help start-ups flourish in more difficult contexts. in today's rapidly changing world, start-ups give themselves an advantage by joining ecosystems that bring needed resources together for the journey.

Similarly, in more difficult contexts like the one we are navigating, the journey to success cannot be made alone. We need an ecosystem that helps change the odds of success the way businesses change their odds by being a part of ecosystems that foster their growth.

So now we need a new mental model. Now we must see all the pivots and innovation that must happen in our lives as an integral part of the game of life, not an exception. Let's reverse how we see this. It is no longer a bug; it is a feature of our lives. So instead of assuming that our lives will stay on a steady path upward and that perhaps we will need one-off development to get us back on track in an otherwise stable life, we should manage our lives in ecosystems designed to smooth the ride in a more volatile world and bring us as individuals the same traction that business ecosystems bring to start-ups.

SHIFT PARADIGM: FROM THE SINGULAR JOURNEY TO THE ECOSYSTEM VIEW OF GROWTH AND SUCCESS

Given the more challenging context we face, we must change our paradigm of how we view the journey to success to that of start-ups and small businesses. We no longer play the game alone; instead, we play the game in a full ecosystem that allows us to leverage the people, information, and resources to help us succeed and continually innovate across our lifetime.

For growth, we must now lead and manage ourselves like businesses, not consumers. This also means that we need to create multiple bridges in our nonlinear journey. We now will need to bridge from doing a job as an employee to being an intrapreneur. Even if you are working as an employee, you must think differently; being your own CEO is how you need to create your own security and paths to sustainability while also building your mental and lifestyle fitness.

You will need to bridge from holding just one job to finding multiple ways to work. You want to diversify your income streams by having more than one gig, including how to grow your business. You want to do so foundationally and sustainably to increase your sense of control and security.

You are also likely going to need to reinvent yourself as a professional. You want to redeploy the professional skills you have developed and build from the professional achievements you have honed. You will be looking to fill in the gaps that are now critical for your success and for creating peace of mind. Being part of an ecosystem also helps with the idea stage of creating your own business. It provides support as you build the back-end infrastructure you will need to incubate and grow your business sustainably.

Ecosystems can provide the accelerants to extend your reach and hasten your results by using your context to your advantage, accelerating your growth to counter the speed of change. Ecosystems for success should be replicated throughout your lifespan to increase your exposure to the resources, networks, etc., that you will need to grow and make in-game adjustments across your lifetime.

11

CHAPTER 11

BLUEPRINT 5

FROM 20TH CENTURY EDUCATION TO 21ST CENTURY PREPARATION

We must prepare students for a future we can neither describe nor predict.
—DAVID WARLICK

THE MASTERY BLUEPRINT

The Mastery Blueprint taught us that a good education was the ticket to success. It was supposed to guarantee entry into the middle class and ascendancy up the ladder of success and keep us from falling backward in our quality or standard of living during tougher times. So, it was supposed to provide a leg up and to be an insulator for not falling through cracks.

WHAT WE LEARNED

20th century education, built for industrial times, taught us how to acquire information. In the industrial economy—which was largely based on tangible assets—rote learning, collecting information, and mastering what was known were the goals so that we could become more productive and experts through repetition and mastery of the known. In the 20th century, we went from student to employer to consumer, and education was supposed to provide a relatively seamless path to success.

 ## CONTEXT MATTERS

A degree no longer automatically leads to a good job or a good life.

We have gone from a 20th century industrial-based economy to a 21st century knowledge-based economy. We went from an economic paradigm built on tangible assets and powered by what we currently know to an economic paradigm built on intellectual assets and powered by what we *can* know. Therefore, 20th century education is preparing for a time that no longer exists.

In the old world of work, the jobs and industries we trained for did not disappear quickly, but times are no longer static. Traditional education does not prepare us for the many ways to work beyond becoming an employee, and degrees are not necessarily mapped to creating value in our fast-changing world of work.

Going to college no longer automatically equals obtaining a good-paying job, because it teaches students just to get a job in the old world rather than prepare for the world as it is. The cost has increased relative to the value being provided for students because it is now less connected to the skills in demand and to the requisite experiences that can help students turn knowledge into in-demand skills. Therefore, even if they do everything right, many students graduate with too much debt without creating a foothold in the world of work that helps them launch their careers.

WE ARE IN A CONSTANTLY CHANGING CONTEXT, SO WE MUST NAVIGATE DIFFERENTLY—EDUCATION MUST NOW HAVE A DIFFERENT PURPOSE

Education as it is does not prepare us for most jobs in this new economy, nor does it prepare us for navigating the world itself. We are prepared to be employees and consumers, but we now need new skills to adapt, to be innovative and dynamic to grow in constant change, not just prepared to be an employee.

We need to learn to lead ourselves economically and personally to navigate life in a more challenging context in the short run. Our education teaches academic literacy, but now we need multiple literacies to navigate life.

Previously, we did not have to learn to lead and manage our lives in the way we must learn to do now. We did not have to lead and manage our lives in a rapidly changing world. Traditional education teaches us how to accumulate information, not lead, manage, and innovate throughout our lives.

Information and learning do not equal preparation for life. We need lifelong preparation to be dynamic in order to innovate as needed. It must prepare us for change and the future. Since the game is constantly changing, it must prepare us to lead and manage ourselves as a business, not as a consumer.

True control over our lives is now about how well we can lead and manage our lives in this more challenging context of uncertainty, change, and disruption. Traditional education no longer prepares us for, nor does it guarantee, success in life. Therefore, we are educated but unprepared. We now must prepare differently to lead and manage ourselves so we can play the game differently and innovate throughout our lives.

SHIFT PARADIGM FROM THIS...

TO THIS:

THE INNOVATOR BLUEPRINT

21ST CENTURY PREPARATION

A good degree is a good thing, but it is not a guarantee for success. We need to change the paradigm of education, since that was built for an industrial age. We must move beyond the old ways of educating ourselves for a bygone era. We are currently trained to learn and repeat the right answer as a sign of mastery. Yet now we need to be trained to see context, seek strategies, and have dynamism. We must be prepared to see what can be, not just what is.

> We now must prepare differently to lead and manage ourselves so we can play the game differently and innovate throughout our lives.

So, we need to switch our paradigm from 20th century education to 21st century preparation. Preparation must also include playing the game differently in order to grow securely and acquiring the foundational skills and fitness to grow sustainably.

 **NEW GOAL**

Our goal must be to be prepared to innovate more dynamically.

THE BASICS

Preparation must provide a path and leg up to the ways to use skills, ways to work, and how to navigate life. The goal should be to increase dynamism, not just to increase an accumulation of knowledge. We need skills to manage our lives holistically, now and in the future.

Beyond the ABCs as being foundational to our education, we need to see the big five pillars of preparation as being foundational to our readiness to navigate life successfully. To win the new game of life, we must learn how to play five games, not just one. To play under constant pressure and to perform at the elite level, like athletes and CEOs, we must master the Future of Work game, the Business of You game, the Life Fitness game, the Mental game, and the Life Navigation game.

THE 21ST CENTURY PREPARATION ROAD MAP

 ## LEVEL 1

20TH CENTURY EDUCATION

The previous era said that just by getting a degree, you were ready to achieve your dreams.

BLUEPRINT 5: FROM 20TH CENTURY EDUCATION TO 21ST CENTURY PREPARATION

We were judged before by how well we conformed to the standards, how well we could master rote learning, and how well we could regurgitate information. We were rewarded for academic intelligence in order to be employees. Education was seen as something that happened in a very prescribed time frame, and it was all inside the school walls. We played one game: the student-to-employee game.

A good degree is a good thing, but it is not a guarantee for success, so we need to change the paradigm of education, since that was built for an industrial age that was about academic literacy only. Our formal education does not train us for daily living today.

Preparedness is no longer about having a diploma in hand. Now, the question is whether we are prepared for life, so now we need a different preparation.

We need to prepare ourselves, not just educate ourselves, for life. Life is now more like a game that requires broad training. The game of life is a sport, but we were only taught to play with one shot. We need new, different game skills—the ability to prepare and anticipate the unexpected and not just master what we've learned in one season of life. In this new context of the new normal, we all need to learn how to navigate life basics. Life literacy is no longer just the degree; it is all the future-ready skills and literacies we all need. This is about being future prepared.

We learned one shot, but that is no longer enough to actually win the game. We learned how to play by making the plays on an employer's court, but we never needed or learned the all-around skills, fitnesses, and literacies to know how to navigate. We now need to be equipped to navigate the new world, which means to anticipate what is ahead in uncertainty and to be able to make better decisions even under imperfect conditions. The level of equipping we all need is very different.

 **LEVEL 2**

PREPARATION TO NAVIGATE LIFE

NEW CLASSROOMS

When we think of education, we typically think of the learning that happens inside classroom walls. But now we need to emphasize experiences on many fronts beyond the traditional classroom. Preparation is about learning five games in four different classrooms. You need skill-based experiences to turn knowledge into actual skills. Work experience must be a classroom, not just a destination to build critical skills and networks.

You need performance-based training to win an overall championship when there is greater pressure. When you are under pressure, you must build resilience and learn to perform at a higher level. This performance under pressure is necessary for life success. To compete in this new game of life, the training and life lessons that come from sports help us mentally, interpersonally, and strategically and helps us develop our leadership skills.

Life itself is a classroom that helps us build environmental awareness to navigate the world and achieve better outcomes. This new paradigm shift from education to preparation will now allow us to manage our present and our future even in uncertainty so that we are prepared to meet our goals.

NEW GOALS

In our old view of education, the purpose of our narrower education-to-career goal was success as primarily defined by material plenty. Now, in our new view of preparation, the purpose is to prepare us for our redefined view of success, which is obtaining simultaneous health, wealth, and happiness.

HAPPINESS: SUITING UP FOR THE GAME

FIGURE 11.1: FOCUS ON HAPPINESS

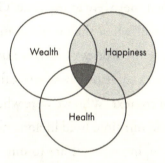

Success redefined is at the intersection of health, wealth, and happiness.

LEARNING PERSONAL AND LIFE INTELLIGENCE TO BEGIN YOUR LIFE

Before we play any game, we need to be properly suited up. In the old game of life, suiting up was simply showing up for school and preparing academically. We never learned who we were standing still. We never learned who we were outside of academic accomplishment. After being unhappy despite our accomplishments, we went in search of happiness. But by then, it became a deep excavation project to find who we were beneath all of what we had accumulated without ever properly suiting up for the game.

Personal intelligence, discovering our center of gravity, and locating our true north such as our core strengths, values, goals, and life vision are key life locators. These life animators help bring the happiness and meaning that we seek in our lives. Knowing our strengths is also critical to being ready to play the games.

When I was a Gallup Strengths Coach, one of the things I would always do before presenting executives with the results of their StrengthsFinder assessment was to ask them to tell me stories of when they believed they were at their finest. I wanted them to tell me stories in their life about when they were in the zone. One caveat: preferably, they should be stories of when they were younger. Not professional stories. That is because the stories of how we use our core strengths, when we are happiest and at our best, are often seen most clearly outside a professional context. Who we were when we were young and how we chose to spend our time hold lifelong clues to our happiness. Suiting up means bringing who we are to our consciousness so that we can live more of those kinds of experiences.

WEALTH: PLAYING THE FUTURE OF WORK AND BUSINESS OF YOU GAMES

FIGURE 11.2: FOCUS ON WEALTH

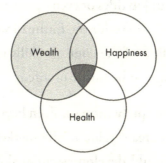

Success redefined is at the intersection of health, wealth, and happiness.

THE FUTURE OF WORK GAME: THE NEW ABCS OF SKILLS, EXPERIENCES, AND NETWORKS

Future-focused skills. We now need to prepare to learn the skills to help us navigate. We need to prepare like athletes to run our own race, like CEOs and innovators. We need to prepare to navigate, innovate, and adapt, not just to take a job and do rote work. We need new intelligences and skills. Education trained you to be a student, then an employee, and then a consumer. This is the mastery blueprint. Now, we need to train to be leaders, managers, and innovators in our lives and our businesses.

This means that we need to not just obtain a degree. Being prepared to create value is skill based, as knowledge is more and more commoditized. We need to translate information into skills that allow us to create value in the marketplace and obtain the essential skills that are uniquely human. The purpose is to have many ways to work and lead, manage, and innovate your life.

You must also connect skills to essential experiences and networks to build essential capital to achieve your long-term goals more sustainably. To grow securely and more stable, we no longer see ourselves through the lens of our job titles or even our degrees. Skills are the new currency that can position us for the future of work and will position us for success regardless of the context. Skills must be connected to ways to make a living and be future proofed.

Essentials skills—uniquely human. Even beyond transferable skills that position you to create value in the marketplace and that have market ROI, you should develop essential skills that are uniquely human so that they are not replaceable by machines or AI.

Thinking skills, such as critical thinking, creative thinking, and problem-solving, and interpersonal skills, such as communication, empathy, and collaboration, will always be in demand.

Experiences and networks. This 21st century preparation relies on critical experiences and relationships. Preparation must now be about a wealth of experiences in and out of school from the earliest years that put individuals at the center, actively engaged in connected, real-world learning that helps develop those critical capacities and provides broad exposure to people, opportunities, and networks. These experiences can range from after-school and summer experiences to apprenticeships and internships.

THE BUSINESS OF YOU GAME

We need leadership and management skills to run ourselves like a business, not like a consumer. This means we can't just manage our careers. We need to see the full court and have full game intelligence. So, in other words, we can't just focus on growth; we need the key literacies to play the game in a way that allows us to build our life infrastructure so that we can provide our own stability and security so we can succeed and thrive sustainably.

To master the Business of You game, we must learn all the ways to work and make a living. We traditionally learn how to be an employee, but we also must learn how to be an entrepreneur, how to work as a consultant, and how to work in the gig economy so that we can diversify the sources of our income and career smoothly in a nonlinear world.

The Business of You game is about learning how to build your own economic engine and treating yourself with the same discipline that businesses do by being financially literate, knowing how to build life infrastructure, managing your money, creating your own safety nets and economic security to build financial capital to grow and build wealth, managing risk, and figuring out how to grow and control your future.

HEALTH: PLAYING THE LIFE FITNESS GAME

FIGURE 11.3: FOCUS ON HEALTH

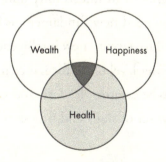

Success redefined is at the intersection of health, wealth, and happiness.

PLAYING THE LIFE FITNESS GAME

To manage our more challenging personal economy and the impact of stress in our life, we need a higher level of fitness. We must develop the key fitness that will allow us to improve our well-being, maintain health, and maintain our standard and quality of living even in uncertainty. By knowing how to grow your well-being, strength, resilience, and endurance to play the game over multiple rounds, you can increase your healthspan, not just your lifespan.

We have all learned the importance of incorporating physical fitness into our lifestyle. Now, we must expand our understanding of lifestyle fitness to prioritize financial, mental, career, and lifestyle fitness as part of our healthy lifestyle.

LEVEL 3

MASTERING THE MENTAL GAME

Education is based on a model in which you must limit your choices to one major for the purpose of one degree. Preparation is about creating value and growth in uncertainty and constant disruption. And just like we now need new fundamentals beyond our ABCs to prepare, we now need to develop new intelligences and mindsets that are required for a higher level of performance in uncertainty.

Now we need to be creators, leaders, and managers of ourselves, which requires a new set of skills and fitness and training to play an entirely new game.

BLUEPRINT 5: FROM 20TH CENTURY EDUCATION TO 21ST CENTURY PREPARATION

FROM CONVERGENT AND CRYSTALLIZED TO DIVERGENT AND FLUID

The skills we needed before trained us to be employees and students and then consumers. It rewarded rote learning.

Rewarded for learning what to think. We were rewarded for memorizing the one right answer to a problem and accumulating knowledge based on known answers to previously solved problems.

Our educational system is based on convergent thinking. Convergent thinking focuses on reaching one well-defined solution to a problem. Convergent thinking involves finding the single correct answer to a well-defined problem. This type of thinking is best suited for tasks that involve logic as opposed to creativity, such as answering multiple-choice tests or solving a problem where you know there are no other possible solutions.

This convergent thinking builds largely crystallized intelligence, which is accumulated knowledge you can recall as needed. School testing of learned facts and job-candidate testing of software knowledge are examples of crystallized knowledge assessments. To increase your crystallized intelligence, you simply need to acquire new knowledge. Education and experience can help it take root in your long-term memory.

The skills we needed before trained us to be employees and students and then consumers. But there are no longer any safe harbors. No more rewards for learning a body of knowledge and following the well-worn paths of safe and predictable career paths.

In this Mastery Blueprint for thinking, we learn to accumulate knowledge to solve known problems, not to innovate to solve new ones, which requires a new kind of thinking to train to play an entirely new game. What is taught does not prepare us for most jobs currently, nor does it prepare us for managing our life in uncertainty.

Rewarded for how to think. The creative innovation we now need comes from learning divergent thinking. Divergent thinking is the opposite of convergent thinking and involves more creativity. Divergent thinking is producing multiple solutions to a problem in which the product is not completely determined by the information. So, divergent thinking concentrates on generating many alternative responses, including original, unexpected, or unusual ideas. Thus, divergent thinking is associated with creativity.

While convergent thinking helps to build crystallized intelligence, divergent thinking helps to build fluid intelligence. Fluid intelligence is your ability to learn, assess, and navigate new situations. While problem-solving uses both crystallized and fluid intelligences, in fluid intelligence, *how* to think in order to generate novel responses is more important than *what* to think.

We associate developing crystallized intelligence with traditional classroom learning. In contrast, developing fluid intelligence requires a more comprehensive approach. Research has found that it reflects the health and fitness of your brain. So, to increase this type of intelligence, you'll need to nourish it through a good diet, regular exercise, stress reduction, adequate sleep, and mindfulness training. Instead of just accumulating information, brain fitness would include activities such as learning a new language, playing strategy games like chess, engaging in cognitive training, changing your routines, learning new skills and hobbies, socializing more, learning a musical instrument, challenging yourself mentally, and using your mind to remember things instead of relying on apps and other devices to think for you.

 **LEVEL 4**

MASTERING THE LIFE NAVIGATION GAME

While the previous games were about mastering key skills and intelligences that allow you to play multiple games throughout your lifetime, the Life Navigation game is about mastering the more challenging context, or ecosystem, itself.

People are facing constant economic and mental health headwinds—overall extremes, sea changes, disruptions, tectonic shifts. We must learn how to navigate life to become future proofed, which now includes managing constant change and uncertainty as well as a more challenging personal economy in the short run. Future proofed is being prepared for tomorrow. This new paradigm of navigation will now allow us to manage our present and future even in uncertainty so that we are prepared to meet our goals: what you need to act in uncertainty.

MULTIPLE INTELLIGENCES MUST COME TOGETHER TO PLAY THE GAME OF LIFE NAVIGATION

Life navigation is about thinking contextually, divergently, strategically, and innovatively. It involves learning to have the big-picture skills to strategically manage multiple pieces of information simultaneously, anticipate what will happen, and respond accordingly.

ESSENTIAL LIFE NAVIGATION SKILLS

Life is coming at us fast. The constant friction around us is causing stress, anxiety, etc. It is no longer a smooth walk, and this makes us feel fragile. Our context of uncertainty is now a part of our backdrop, so the key to managing the external friction that is now part of the backdrop and still being mobile is knowing how to move in uncertainty, not wait for certainty.

Life navigation skills allow you to be context informed so that you can navigate the world around you while being able to be prepared for tomorrow. Life navigation is about scanning and pattern spotting. We must learn to horizon scan, perform trend analysis, and synthesize information and skills from many sources to distinguish between signal and noise in the sea of information that floods us. It is the knowledge of how to spot trends and gather information to make good decisions, not just rely on the strong opinions and influence of others.

Life navigation skills include constant environmental scans to monitor headwinds and tailwinds and performing SWOT analyses to navigate uncertainty, hedge risk, and grow. You must scan constantly and play the odds. In a SWOT analysis, you're looking for both opportunities and risks. You must be able to mitigate and reduce risks. You must assess whether the upside is worth the downside in uncertainty. For example, attending college and racking up debt should not be automatic moves we all make. We must assess the upside with the downside of too much debt. We must ask ourselves, "Can I mitigate it, and can I eliminate it?"

Life navigation also involves being agile enough to make multiple plays and pivot when needed to account for uncertainty and absorb shocks, because you have accounted for the inevitable periods of contraction.

LIFELONG DESIGN THINKING FOR LIFELONG INNOVATION

Life navigation as a lifelong strategy requires us to become lifelong innovators and problem solvers. We must prepare for lifelong navigation and innovation by lifting from our thinking ABCs of convergent and divergent thinking for creative problem-solving. This kind of problem-solving is the basis for human-centered design (HCD) thinking, which is a nonlinear, iterative process that teams use to tackle ill-defined or unknown problems. It is an approach to problem-solving that puts the person at the heart of the process, and while it was originally derived to design products more innovatively, we as people can learn from this methodology and adopt the key principles of human-centered design in order to continually innovate in our own lives.

FIGURE 11.4: THE DESIGN THINKING PROCESS

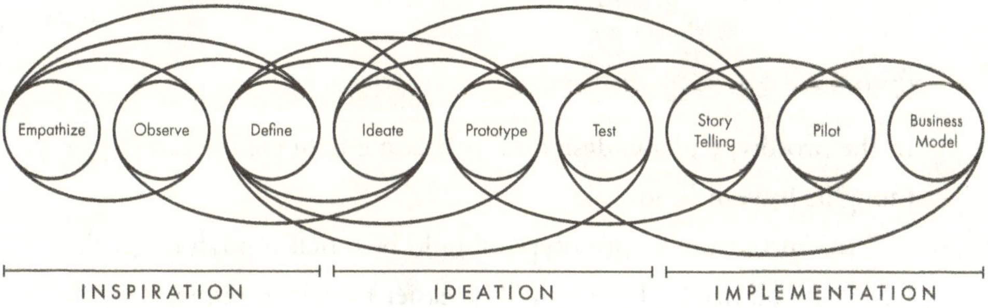

There are three main phases in a design thinking process: inspiration, ideation, and implementation.

Inspiration

The human-centered design process is, at its core, about understanding people's thinking and why. Understanding people, what motivates them, and why is critical for a design thinker's success. As we apply this inspiration phase of design thinking to our own lives, we see that the basis of true-life innovation begins with deep self-understanding and personal and life intelligence. This critical life start sets up continued lifelong opportunities for innovative life solutions.

Ideation

To ideate is to generate solutions. The ideation phase is considered the gateway to innovation because it's not just about coming up with one correct answer—it's also about exploring possibilities by being broad and diverse so we can choose from many viable pathways as our journey progresses. Similarly, one key purpose of our educational preparation must be divergent thinking. Not only must we learn how to ideate as a way to solve problems; we also must be able to pair what we learn about ourselves with many ways to innovate and create value in the world continuously.

Prototype

In the prototype phase, design ideas become tangible instead of just thoughts in your head.

Initial versions of prototypes should be quick enough to get the feedback you need. This way, it'll be easier to iterate, refine, discard, or pivot based on discovering precisely what works and what could be improved. Similarly, your educational preparation should not be narrowed to one major, nor should you just accumulate knowledge and call that ready. You should prototype with after-school and summer experiences as well as internships and apprenticeships.

BLUEPRINT 5: FROM 20TH CENTURY EDUCATION TO 21ST CENTURY PREPARATION

Implementation

As you test and implement your life solutions, you should continue to revisit and use the Life and Business of You™ models that you have created for yourself. This will allow you to implement many life and work solutions within your chosen business models based on your personal and life intelligence.

Storytelling

Your career portfolio brings coherence to your story of yourself as you continue to test, prototype, and innovate throughout your life. When creating your design journey, your job title no longer holds it together—rather, it's your story throughline, your why. It is the way to tell your story to yourself and others so it hangs together no matter how diverse the plays may seem on the surface. The throughline is what helps you effectively innovate and connect the dots of your own journey.

PART 3

DEFINING MOMENTS

12

CHAPTER 12

THE FUTURE IS HUMAN

*From what we get, we can make a living;
what we give, however, makes a life.*
—ARTHUR ASHE

THE AMERICAN DREAM REVISITED

The American Dream, originally espoused by James Truslow Adams in 1931, animated our nation and the world with a unifying vision that with hard work, we could transcend the circumstances of our birth and live to our fullest, and our kids would be better off than we were.

Not only did the original dream evolve into being defined by what we need to have, such as a house and cars, to achieve it, but research on the trends in upward mobility showed that in 1940, a child had a 90 percent chance of earning more than their parents. In 1955, it was a 70 percent chance, but by the 1990s, the chance was 50 percent—no better than a coin toss.

BEATING THE ODDS

This new view of the American Dream, the new view of health, wealth, and happiness, is now about who we must be to achieve it, not what we must have. The new life blueprint for our redefined view of success is a profound shift from how we understood our roles within the old blueprint to the life leadership, management, and constant innovation required for our new Innovator Blueprint. This new blueprint gets us to the success, health, and happiness we really desire, particularly in a constantly changing world.

FROM BEATING THE ODDS TO CHANGING THE ODDS

While the American Dream is an articulation of the hopes and aspirations of individuals within our nation, we currently do not measure human success as a nation. We measure other forms of success that, while critical, are not the same as human success.

WHOSE DREAM?

We followed career paths and emptied ourselves to succeed so that we would have a chance at living our own dreams and finding our own happiness. Yet our national success is largely measured by GDP, which is approximately 70 percent consumer spending.

We are more than consumers.

The sum total of our lived experience as individuals, and our human success collectively, is not simply how much we spend or how well we are holding up the economy. We want to do more than just pay bills and meet our obligations. We want to work hard, knowing that our hard work will move us toward realizing our own dreams in the long run, while we have enough to enjoy our everyday life in the short run and still be able to look forward to the future with confidence and optimism.

WHAT WE MEASURE MATTERS

Our national success metrics do not measure our actual lives. They do not measure our personal standard or quality of living, our personal and economic well-being, or our progress toward our own American Dream. We therefore need to broaden how we measure national success to include human success.

A HUMAN VIEW OF SUCCESS

We need a new view of success that centers our human needs, goals, and gaps from a human perspective. To shift our paradigm to attain a human view of success:

- The future of how we view and measure success must be human centered so that we redefine and reinvent the fading American Dream.
- The future of how we work toward success must be human centered to reinvent the broken career ladder to success.
- The future of how we navigate our more complex world must be sustainable so that we can grow toward the health, wealth, and happiness we seek.
- The future of education must be human-centered preparation for leading and managing ourselves in response to our complex world.

To fulfill this vision of human success, we must reimagine and rebuild what is currently broken in our current path to success, and we must rethink and measure human well-being and sustainability.

WE MUST REIMAGINE AND REBUILD

We currently do not discuss holistically or account for the historical and structural shifts that have resulted in the broken path to the American Dream, which is now broken at all stages.

1. **PREPARATION 2030**

   We must commit to ensuring that by 2030, every student will have access to all the key skills, literacies, and fitness that move us from 20th century education to the essential future-forward literacies we all now need to navigate life and that allow us to be dynamic and adapt to the future.

2. **BUILDING A NEW PSYCHOLOGICAL CONTRACT**

   While the 20th century social contract no longer exists, we must construct a new 21st century psychological contract that restores the basic workplace psychological safety required to shift the paradigm from transactional to a relationship of mutual interdependence.

WE MUST RETHINK AND MEASURE

The high volatility and uncertainty of our journey now mean that the national measures of economic health do not accurately portray our personal health and well-being. Our new American Dream includes our ability to build and sustain our personal and economic well-being, so we must also measure this nationally.

1. **THE ECONOMY IS PERSONAL**

    We must commit to ensuring that by 2030, along with the traditional measures of national economic success, we also measure the changing context, headwinds, and realities in which the average person operates in order to measure the health of the personal economy.

2. **PERSONAL SUSTAINABILITY**

    We don't just want to live longer; we want to live healthier in all aspects of our lives. We therefore need a more human-centered frame and measure of human health that captures our underlying well-being and sustainability and encompasses our lived experience so we can lengthen our financial, mental, career, and lifestyle healthspan.

THE FUTURE MUST BE HUMAN

If the new American Dream is now about how we can grow and thrive even in disruption and therefore beat the odds of success, then changing the odds of success is about creating a new story altogether of how we can fulfill our potential as a dynamic nation.

It is about telling ourselves a new story by seeing the power we all have right where we stand to bridge the gap between where we are today and where we must be in the future through a narrative of personal and national purpose.

In 1931, two years after the start of the Great Depression, the worst economic downturn in history, the idea of an American Dream, a bold new vision that created hope in a time of darkness, was born. While it might seem highly dissonant that such a lofty aspiration and ideal was born amid the worst downturn, what is true is that in times of great challenge, there is always also great opportunity.

THE DISRUPTORS

Though it is tempting to see only the challenges, in those moments there is also an even greater story of those who take the lead and find solutions amid what feels like chaos to many. That is because whenever there are major challenges like the ones we currently face, a new generation of disruptors always emerges to help break down old boundaries and ways of thinking and operating.

They do so because Pivotal Moments, while difficult, are also Defining Moments. When we face life-defining moments, we are forced to detach ourselves from the past since we can no longer stay in the familiar, and we must look for solutions in places we never thought we would. By shifting our paradigm, Pivotal Moments can simultaneously be the most difficult and liberating moments that we face. Therefore, we must believe in the power of Defining Moments.

So here we stand at a crossroads, because underlying our need to rebuild the broken path to the American Dream or to rethink and measure our lived health and well-being is a deeper crisis of imagination. The choice is each of ours to make, because while no one can do everything, everyone can do something. We must, therefore, also believe in the power of meeting the moment to bring forth solutions and partnerships that lift higher to cocreate a brighter future for ourselves and future generations.

WHERE TO FROM HERE?

If you would like to continue your journey with us by downloading the discussion guides, please visit:

HTTPS:BLUEPRINTGLOBAL.COM

Through our human-centered research and design lab, we have created a new category and industry of solutions to bridge the gap between what we used to do and how we now must prepare, navigate, lead, manage, and constantly innovate to sustain our success in this context of change and disruption. Our solutions are the full ecosystem of what we all need but have not yet been taught anywhere.

TAKE THE HEALTH AND STRESS ASSESSMENT

Map your financial, mental, career, and lifestyle health and fitness to get started on your personal sustainability journey.

ACCESS OUR LIFE SCHOOL

Our Life School media help you close the gap between your formal classroom education and the life preparation you need today.

THE NEW LIFE BLUEPRINT

JOIN OUR BUSINESS OF YOU ACCELERATOR™

Train, incubate, and accelerate in the paradigm-shifting, holistic ecosystem that will ensure your success across your lifespan.

LEARN ABOUT OUR CONSULTING SERVICES

Our proprietary Blueprint 360 strategy and consulting process is designed for professionals at all stages of growth and transition.

JOIN OUR NATIONAL INITIATIVES

Our multiyear national initiatives address the critical gaps between our 20th century paradigms and what we must do to move us into 21st century thinking to succeed.

ACKNOWLEDGMENTS

There are some books that you choose to write, and others that choose you.

This book chose me.

The New Life Blueprint is the product of my more than decade-long quest to understand how the forces of change shape and reshape our lives.

Right after the 2008 Great Recession, I was simultaneously serving as a board member of the Federal Reserve Board Tenth District and as the CEO of a nonprofit organization. This unique perspective allowed me to view up close both our national vulnerability and our personal vulnerability. This was when it became clear to me that the world was changing in profound ways but that we were unprepared to navigate this new reality. This truth gripped me.

While this quest has shaped my professional career over the last decade, my interest in this topic and the changing American Dream is also deeply personal. That is because I am the first generation in my family to grow up in this country. My family and I are originally from Panama, so my first language is Spanish. My parents sacrificed a great deal for my brother and me to ensure we had the opportunities they did not have. So, being the first generation in my family to have been educated in this country, I know what a gift it was to have the chance to reach beyond what my parents imagined was possible for me.

Therefore, it is with the deepest love and gratitude that I thank my parents for one of the greatest gifts one could ever receive—opportunity. While I can never truly repay them for all they have done, given, and sacrificed on my behalf, I can pay it forward.

My life mission, as expressed through this book, is my attempt to pay it forward by helping others live their American Dream just as I was given the opportunity to live mine.

Though this book was a long time in the making, it would not have been possible without the support of the talented professionals at Forbes Books. Thank you to Bonnie Hearn-Hill, Heidi Scott, Annie LaGreca, Elizabeth Kennedy, Megan Elger, and Elizabeth Brueggemann.

You all have my sincere appreciation for walking this journey with me.

ABOUT THE AUTHORS

DR. NATALIA PEART IS THE CEO AND FOUNDER OF BLUEPRINT GLOBAL, LLC.

She is a multi-hyphenate psychologist, business and career consultant, best-selling author, speaker, and *Forbes* contributor. Throughout her career, she has worked as a clinical psychologist, a leadership and performance consultant for Fortune 1000 companies to small businesses, an executive and personal consultant, a foundation chief officer, and a nonprofit CEO. She is the author of *Future Proofed: The New Rules of Success in Work & Life for Our Modern World*, an Amazon bestseller in five categories.

She is a SXSW 2021 presenter and has been featured in various media outlets, including *Harvard Business Review*, *New York Times*, FOX, *Wall Street Journal*, *Barron's*, Yahoo Finance, *Oprah Magazine*, *Black Enterprise*, Glassdoor, Elite Daily, and Thrive Global. She has also spoken at events ranging from small group workshops to three-thousand-person events.

She has served on the Federal Reserve Board, 10th District, and earned her BA with honors in psychology from Brown University, her PhD in clinical/community psychology from the University of Maryland, and completed her clinical internship at Boston Children's Hospital/Harvard Medical School.

CHRISTOPHER BURGE IS THE COO AND COFOUNDER OF BLUEPRINT GLOBAL, LLC.

Prior to this role, Chris enjoyed a successful career in the financial services industry. As a former Wall Street executive, he began his career at the prestigious Salomon Brothers investment firm. He spent his career helping the country's largest portfolio managers, including Prudential Insurance Company, manage their fixed income portfolios. He was one of only six people in their competitive sales and trading class. He was promoted to vice president at the age of twenty-five and became a millionaire before the age of thirty.

Chris is known as a gifted communicator who has always been motivated by helping people maximize their potential. He has spoken in front of audiences ranging from thirty to three thousand and has been profiled in publications such as *Bloomberg Businessweek*. He is a graduate of Brown University with a Bachelor of Arts degree in economics. He is a lifelong athlete. At Brown, he was a basketball team captain and is currently an avid golfer.

REFERENCES

Adams, James Truslow. *The Epic of America*. Boston, Mass.: Little, Brown, and Company, 1931.

"America Retains 'Rent Burdened' Status." Moody's. November 2023. https://www.moodys.com/web/en/us/about/insights/data-stories/q3-2023-rental-affordability.html.

"America's Rental Housing 2024." Harvard Joint Center for Housing Studies. https://www.jchs.harvard.edu/americas-rental-housing-2024.

Associated Press. "Consumers Are Fighting Back against 'Greedflation' at Grocery Stores." *Fast Company*. February 2024. https://www.fastcompany.com/91038066/inflation-consumers-push-back-price-gouging.

Belkin, Douglas. "Why Americans Have Lost Faith in the Value of College." *Wall Street Journal*. January 2024. https://www.wsj.com/us-news/education/why-americans-have-lost-faith-in-the-value-of-college-b6b635f2.

Berger, Chloe. "Gen X Is Actually More Worried about Retirement than Boomers." *Fortune*. February 2024. https://fortune.com/2024/02/27/gen-x-retirement-anxiety-more-worried-than-baby-boomers/.

Bhattarai, Abha. "Less Money, Less House: How Market Forces Are Reshaping the American Home." *Washington Post*. March 2024. https://www.washingtonpost.com/business/2024/03/10/smaller-new-houses-afforable/.

Bowman, Bridget. "'Mourning in America': Poll Finds Pessimistic Voters." NBC News. November 2023. https://www.nbcnews.com/meet-the-press/meetthepressblog/mourning-america-poll-finds-pessimistic-voters-rcna126180.

Burke, Lilah. "Half of Graduates End up Underemployed—What Does That Mean for Colleges?" *Higher Ed Dive*. March 2024. https://www.highereddive.com/news/half-of-graduates-end-up-underemployed-what-does-that-mean-for-colleges/710836/#:~:text=They%20issued%20a%20big%20finding,number%20only%20drops%20to%2045%25.

"Business Cycle Dating Committee Announcement June 8, 2020." National Bureau of Economic Research. June 2020. https://www.nber.org/news/business-cycle-dating-committee-announcement-june-8-2020.

Cerullo, Megan. "More than Half of College Graduates Are Working in Jobs That Don't Require Degrees." MoneyWatch. February 2024. https://www.cbsnews.com/news/college-grads-jobs-underemployed/#:~:text=For%20example%2C%20securing%20an%20internship,to%20get%2C%22%20Sigelman%20said.

CFR.org Editors. "Is Rising Student Debt Harming the U.S. Economy?" Council on Foreign Relations. April 2024. https://www.cfr.org/backgrounder/us-student-loan-debt-trends-economic-impact.

Raj Chetty et al. "The Fading American Dream: Trends in Absolute Income Mobility Since 1940." Opportunity Insights. December 2016. https://opportunityinsights.org/national_trends/.

"Consumer Prices up 9.1 percent over the Year Ended June 2022, Largest Increase in 40 Years." U.S. Bureau of Labor Statistics. July 2022. https://www.bls.gov/opub/ted/2022/consumer-prices-up-9-1-percent-over-the-year-ended-june-2022-largest-increase-in-40-years.htm.

Crist, Carolyn. "Nearly Half of Companies Say They Plan to Eliminate Bachelor's Degree Requirements in 2024." *Higher Ed Dive*. December 2023. https://www.highereddive.com/news/nearly-half-of-companies-plan-to-eliminate-bachelors-degree-requirements/702277/.

Dickler, Jessica. "56 Million Americans Have Been in Credit Card Debt for at Least a Year. 'We Are Seeing Pockets of Trouble,' Expert Says." CNBC. January 2024. https://www.cnbc.com/2024/01/08/56-million-americans-have-been-in-credit-card-debt-for-at-least-a-year.html.

Dickler, Jessica. "Credit Card Balances Spiked in the Third Quarter to a $1.08 Trillion Record. Here's How We Got Here." CNBC. November 2023. https://www.cnbc.com/2023/11/07/credit-card-balances-jump-to-1point08-trillion-record-how-we-got-here.html.

Dickler, Jessica. "In Many Ways, Gen Zers Are Better off than Their Parents Were 30 Years Ago, But Fewer Are Financially Independent—Here's Why." CNBC. January 2024. https://www.cnbc.com/2024/01/27/gen-z-vs-their-parents-how-the-generations-stack-up-financially.html.

Ducharme, Jamie. "Why 'Healthspan' May Be More Important than Lifespan." *TIME*. November 2023. https://time.com/6341027/what-is-healthspan-vs-lifespan/.

Empower Annuity Insurance Company of America. "Financial Happiness." The Currency. July 2024. https://www.empower.com/the-currency/money/research-financial-happiness.

Foster, Sarah. "Survey: In This Economy, the Sign of Financial Success Isn't Being a Millionaire But Living Comfortably, Many Americans Say." Bankrate. May 2024. https://www.bankrate.com/banking/savings/financial-success-survey/#:~:text=%22Survey%3A%20In%20this%20economy%2C,financial%2Dsuccess%2Dsurvey%2F.

Fowers, Alyssa, Emily Guskin, and Scott Clement. "How Americans Define a Middle-Class Lifestyle—And Why They Can't Reach It." *Washington Post*. February 2024. https://www.washingtonpost.com/business/2024/02/15/middle-class-financial-security/.

Fuhrmans, Vanessa and Lindsay Ellis. "Half of College Grads Are Working Jobs That Don't Use Their Degrees." *Wall Street Journal*. February 2024. https://www.wsj.com/lifestyle/careers/college-degree-jobs-unused-440b2abd.

Gallo, Linda. "Speaking of Psychology: The Stress of Money, with Linda Gallo, PhD." American Psychological Association, 2015. https://www.apa.org/news/podcasts/speaking-of-psychology/financial-stress#:~:text=APA's%20latest%20Stress%20in%20America,sources%20can%20affect%20your%20health.

Golden, Lonnie. "Irregular Work Scheduling and Its Consequences." Economic Policy Institute. April 2015. https://www.epi.org/publication/irregular-work-scheduling-and-its-consequences/#:~:text=Irregular%20scheduling,with%20unstable%20work%20shift%20schedules.

"The Great Gloom: In 2023, Employees Are Unhappier than Ever. Why?" BambooHR. https://www.bamboohr.com/resources/guides/employee-happiness-h1-2023.

Hanson, Melanie. "College Tuition Inflation Rate." Education Data Initiative. August 2023. https://educationdata.org/college-tuition-inflation-rate.

Henry Ford Health Staff. "The Pandemic Skip: What It Is and How to Cope." Henry Ford Health. March 2024. https://www.henryford.com/blog/2024/03/pandemic-skip.

"History of Changes to the Minimum Wage Law." U.S. Department of Labor. https://www.dol.gov/agencies/whd/minimum-wage/history.

Houston, Elaine. "What Are Attributional and Explanatory Styles in Psychology?" PositivePsychology.com. March 2019. https://positive-psychology.com/explanatory-styles-optimism/.

"How LinkedIn Editor-in-Chief Dan Roth Pivoted from Print Journalism to Tech, Plus Top Takeaways from *The Path* Podcast Season 1," *The Path* with Ryan Roslansky. LinkedIn News. November 21, 2023. https://www.linkedin.com/posts/linkedin-news_linear-career-paths-do-not-exist-the-path-activity-7132851168791126016-glt_.

Ito, Aki. "What I Got Wrong about Loyalty at Work." Business Insider. February 2024. https://www.businessinsider.com/work-loyalty-gen-z-millennials-gen-x-boomers-employee-engagement-2024-2.

Johnson Hess, Abigail. "College Costs Have Increased by 169% since 1980—But Pay for Young Workers Is up by Just 19%: Georgetown Report." CNBC. November 2021. https://www.cnbc.com/2021/11/02/the-gap-in-college-costs-and-earnings-for-young-workers-since-1980.html.

Jones, Jeffrey M. "Middle-Class Identification Steady in U.S." Gallup. May 2022. https://news.gallup.com/poll/392708/middle-class-identification-steady.aspx.

Kochhar, Rakesh. "The State of the American Middle Class." Pew Research Center. May 2024. https://www.pewresearch.org/race-and-ethnicity/2024/05/31/the-state-of-the-american-middle-class/.

Lawler, Dave. "Americans Think the American Dream Is Dying." Axios. November 2023. https://www.axios.com/2023/11/25/american-dream-poll-wealth-inequality.

Lenthang, Marlene. "Elmo Opened up about His Viral Feelings Tweet on the 'Today' Show—and Then Larry David Showed Up." NBC News. February 2024. https://www.nbcnews.com/pop-culture/pop-culture-news/-lot-feelings-s-okay-elmo-says-check-friends-huge-response-wellness-tw-rcna136722.

Madeson, Melissa. "Seligman's PERMA+ Model Explained: A Theory of Wellbeing." PositivePsychology.com. February 2017. https://positive-psychology.com/perma-model/.

Malinsky, Gili. "More Americans Say They Are Living Paycheck to Paycheck This Year than in 2023—Here's Why." CNBC. April 2024. https://www.cnbc.com/2024/04/09/most-of-americans-are-living-paycheck-to-paycheck-heres-why.html.

Martin, Annika. "Food Prices and Spending." USDA Economic Research Service. June 2024. https://www.ers.usda.gov/data-products/ag-and-food-statistics-charting-the-essentials/food-prices-and-spending/?topicId=1afac93a-444e-4e05-99f3-53217721a8be.

McWhinney, James. "The Demise of the Defined-Benefit Plan and What Replaced It." Investopedia. May 2024. https://www.investopedia.com/articles/retirement/06/demiseofdbplan.asp.

Menon, Vinod. "20 Years of the Default Mode Network: A Review and Synthesis." Department of Psychiatry & Behavioral Sciences and Department of Neurology & Neurological Sciences, Wu Tsai Neurosciences Institute, Stanford University. August 16, 2023. https://med.stanford.edu/content/dam/sm/scsnl/documents/Neuron_2023_Menon_20_years.pdf.

Minkin, Rachel et al. "Parents, Young Adult Children, and the Transition to Adulthood." Pew Research Center. January 2024. https://www.pewresearch.org/social-trends/2024/01/25/parents-young-adult-children-and-the-transition-to-adulthood/.

Morabito, Charlotte. "Why a $100,000 Income No Longer Buys the American Dream in Most Places." CNBC. April 2024. https://www.cnbc.com/2024/04/16/why-a-100000-salary-no-longer-buys-the-american-dream-in-most-places.html.

Munnell, Alicia H. "More Households Are Prepared for Retirement—But This Good News Might Not Last." Center for Retirement Research at Boston College. July 2024. https://crr.bc.edu/more-households-are-prepared-for-retirement-but-this-good-news-might-last/.

"Nearly Half of U.S. Consumers Earning $100K+ Live Paycheck to Paycheck." PYMNTS. April 2024. https://www.pymnts.com/consumer-finance/2024/nearly-half-of-us-consumers-earning-100k-live-paycheck-to-paycheck/.

"New APA Poll: One in Three Americans Feels Lonely Every Week." American Psychiatric Association. January 2024. https://www.psychiatry.org/news-room/news-releases/new-apa-poll-one-in-three-americans-feels-lonely-e.

"Our Epidemic of Loneliness and Isolation." U.S. Department of Health and Human Services." 2023. https://www.hhs.gov/sites/default/files/surgeon-general-social-connection-advisory.pdf.

Pariona, Amber. "What Was the Digital Revolution?" WorldAtlas. April 2017. https://www.worldatlas.com/articles/what-was-the-digital-revolution.html.

Peart, Natalia. *Future Proofed: The New Rules of Success in Work & Life for Our Modern World*. Beverly, MA, Scrivener Books, 2019.

Peart, Natalia. "Making Work Less Stressful and More Engaging for Your Employees." *Harvard Business Review*. November 2019. https://hbr.org/2019/11/making-work-less-stressful-and-more-engaging-for-your-employees.

Peart, Natalia. "The 12 Most Important Skills You Need to Succeed at Work." *Forbes*. September 2019. https://www.forbes.com/sites/nataliapeart/2019/09/10/the-12-most-important-skills-you-need-to-succeed-at-work/.

Pietrangelo, Ann. "What the Yerkes-Dodson Law Says About Stress and Performance." Healthline. October 2020. https://www.healthline.com/health/yerkes-dodson-law.

Plattner, Hasso. "An Introduction to Design Thinking: PROCESS GUIDE." Institute of Design at Stanford. https://web.stanford.edu/~mshanks/MichaelShanks/files/509554.pdf.

Prakash, Anushna. "Home Buyers Need to Earn $47,000 More than in 2020." Zillow. February 2024. https://www.zillow.com/research/buyers-income-needed-33755/.

"The Productivity–Pay Gap." Economic Policy Institute. October 2022. https://www.epi.org/productivity-pay-gap/.

Raypole, Crystal. "How to Hack Your Hormones for a Better Mood." Healthline. July 2022. https://www.healthline.com/health/happy-hormone.

Royle, Orianna Rosa. "Bad Luck for Fresh-Faced Graduates Who Have Splashed Thousands on a Degree: Job Ads Not Requiring One Is up 90 percent, According to LinkedIn Data." *Fortune*. August 2023. https://fortune.com/2023/08/15/linkedin-employment-recruiting-college-graduates-university-degrees-job-ads/.

Schlifske, John. "Millennials and Gen Zers Are Worried about Outliving Their Savings and Are Turning to Hot-Stock Tips. But a Comprehensive Retirement Plan Drives Better Outcomes." *Fortune*. February 2024. https://fortune.com/2024/02/21/millennials-gen-zers-worried-savings-hot-stock-tips-comprehensive-retirement-plan-outcome-personal-finance/.

"The State of American Jobs." Pew Research Center. October 2016. https://www.pewresearch.org/social-trends/2016/10/06/1-changes-in-the-american-workplace/.

"State of the Global Workplace: 2024." Gallup. https://www.gallup.com/workplace/349484/state-of-the-global-workplace.aspx.

"Stress in America 2023." American Psychological Association. https://www.apa.org/news/press/releases/stress/2023/collective-trauma-recovery#:~:text=When%20reviewing%20this%20year's%20survey,a%20collective%20experience%20among%20Americans.

"Success Index: Misunderstanding the American Dream." Populace.org. July 09, 2023. https://static1.squarespace.com/static/59153bc0e6f2e109b2a85cbc/t/650c26577a79de2ce29b61c8/1695295123767/Success+Index%3A+Misunderstanding+the+American+Dream.

Tergesen, Anne. "More Americans Are Treating Their 401(k)s Like Cash Machines." *The Wall Street Journal.* March 2024. https://www.wsj.com/personal-finance/retirement/more-americans-are-treating-their-401-k-s-like-cash-machines-deaa3f8f.

Whyte, William H. *The Organization Man.* New York, Simon & Schuster, 1956.

Wingard, Jason. "Companies Are Hiring Fewer College Grads—So Why Bother with School?" *Forbes.* April 2024. https://www.forbes.com/sites/jasonwingard/2024/04/30/companies-are-hiring-fewer-college-grads-so-why-bother-with-school/.

Zitner, Aaron. "America Pulls Back from Values That Once Defined It, WSJ-NORC Poll Finds." *Wall Street Journal.* March 2023. https://www.wsj.com/articles/americans-pull-back-from-values-that-once-defined-u-s-wsj-norc-poll-finds-df8534cd.

INDEX

A

Adams, James Truslow, 16–17, 71
agility, 121, 180–181
ambiguity, 57–58. See also VUCA (volatility, uncertainty, complexity, ambiguity)
ambiguous loss, 63–64
American Dream, 15–19, 28, 36–38, 41, 44, 47, 50, 51, 52, 71, 79–80, 213, 214
anticipatory loss, 63–64
anxiety, 6, 52, 61, 150
Ashe, Arthur, 213
assumptions, 35–36
auto loans, 44–45

B

Blueprint Business of You Economic Engine™, 164–165
Blueprint Business of You Growth Engine™, 130–131
Blueprint Four Quadrant Lifestyle Map™, 167
Blueprint Life and Business Model Canvas™, 106, 132
Boomers, 51–52
burnout, 6, 59, 62, 143, 145–146

Business of You game, 20002901
Business of You game playbook, 129–131
Business of You mindset, 175–179, 185–187

C

Capra, Fritjof, 135
career cushioning, 116
career paths, 33–35
career portfolio, 133
career shifting, 124–125
career smoothing, 115–116
career strategy, 125–128
change
agility, 180–181
innovation and, 179–184
pace of, 6, 137
collaboration, 121
collective grief, 63–64
comfort, 69–70
complexity, 57–58. See also VUCA (volatility, uncertainty, complexity, ambiguity)
conditioning, 159–165
Cone of Possibilities, 83
confidence, 27
conscious living, 152
consulting-based business, 118
consumerism, 18, 38, 103, 104
consumer mindset, 173–174, 177
contextual shifts, 41–54

convergent thinking, 203
cost of living, 5, 16, 43
COVID-19 pandemic, 5–6, 58–59, 62–63, 68–69
creativity, 122–123

D

default mode network (DMN), 149
degree-job mismatch, 25. *See also* education
design thinking, 207–209
dexterity, 183
disruptive shifts, 57–64
DMN. *See* default mode network (DMN)
do-it-yourself context, 170–171
dopamine, 158
dynamism, 180, 183, 194

E

economic context, 42–44
economic life picture, 165
education, 20, 22–27, 190, 191–192, 193, 194–195, 202–204
emotional well-being, 61–62
empathy, 122
endorphins, 157, 158
Epic of America (Adams), 16–17
essentialism, 103, 104
experience, paradox of, 183–184
explanatory style, 163–164

F

financial health, 160–161
financial resilience, 164–165
fitness, 146–158
food costs, 16, 43. *See also* inflation
formative life experiences, 60
401(k), 44, 51
four-quadrant lifestyle, 167
Future of Work game playbook, 117–128

G

Gen X, 51
Gen Z, 49–50
globalization, 7, 21, 58
Gould, Elise, 47
Great Recession, 44, 47, 50, 53
grief, 63–64

H

happiness, 19–20, 38, 67–68, 69, 89, 197
HCD. *See* human-centered design (HCD)
health
building foundational, 151–157
connection and, 156–157
conscious living and, 152
core and, 153–154
financial, 160–161

fitness and, 201–202
lifestyle and, 157
mental, 6, 62–63, 68, 160
periodization and, 148–149
pictures of, 165–167
recovery and, 148–149
rest and, 148–149
restoring basic, 147–149
healthspan, 139–146
HERO (hope, efficacy, resilient, optimism), 164
historical shifts, 15–38
home ownership, 18
housing, 16, 18, 43–44
human-centered design (HCD), 207

I

I Am, 105, 176, 177, 178, 181–182
ideation, 208
identity, 107, 175, 178
implementation phase, 209
inflation, 5, 16, 41, 42–44
information-based business, 119
innovation, 83–84, 173, 179–184
Innovator Blueprint, 82, 84, 92, 112, 139, 172–173, 193
inspiration, 207–208
intelligence
career, 93–95
game, 116–131
life, 101–106, 197–198

personal, 96–101, 105, 197–198
interest rates, 16, 41, 48
internships, 26

L

language, understanding and, 160–161
layoffs, 5, 32
leadership, 83–84, 123, 178
life fitness, 201–202
life locators, 97
Life Navigation Game playbook, 131–132
life navigation skills, 206
life plans, 48–49
lifestyle, 157
lifestyle disruption, 60
life vision, 104
likes, loves *vs.*, 102–103
LinkedIn, 33
loans
auto, 44–45
student, 22–23
loneliness, 60
loves, likes v., 102–103

M

major, choice of, 26
management, 83–84

Mastery Blueprint, 15, 21, 22, 67, 81, 82, 84, 135–136, 169–170, 189, 203–204
mental health, 6, 62–63, 68, 160
mental resilience, 162
middle class, 3, 16, 18, 20–21, 22, 41, 46–48
milestones, 49–50, 60
Millennials, 50
minimalism, 103, 104
minimum wage, 43

N

needs, wants *vs.*, 102
negotiation, 123

O

opportunity, 17
organic living and growing, 155–156
Organization Man, The (Whyte), 19
oxytocin, 158

P

pandemic, 5–6, 58–59, 62–63, 68–69
paradigm shifts, 67–73, 91, 130, 152, 171, 186–187
Peart, Natalia, 48–49
pensions, 29
performance, conditioning and, 159–165
periodization, 148–149

PERMA model, 166–167
Personal Leadership, Management, and Innovation, 83–84
personal life picture, 166–167
prices, 41–42, 48. *See also* inflation
priority shifts, 68–69, 91
problem-solving, 123
product-based business, 118
prototype phase, 208

Q

quality of life, 46

R

rent, 43–44. *See also* housing
resilience, 131–132, 161–165
retirement plans, 29. *See also* 401(k)
risk, 28–29
risk security, 131

S

savings, 45
science, technology, engineering, and mathematics (STEM), 26
security, 130–131
self-determination, 176, 181
self-leadership, 178
self-possession, 176, 181
self-realization, 176–177, 181

serotonin, 158
service-based business, 118
short-term navigation context, 80–81
skill(s)
as currency, 120–121
essentials, 200
future-focused, 199–200
greater focus on, 25
life navigation, 206
-need misalignment, 23
small business, 119
social contract, 29–33, 114
social mobility, 17, 37
Social Security, 29, 51–52
start-ups, 185–186
STEM. *See* science, technology, engineering, and mathematics (STEM)
storytelling, 209
stress, 6, 52, 142–146
student loans, 22–23
success, 8–11
Business of You *vs.*, 182–187
education and, 22
foundation of, 101
health and, 141
human view of, 215–216
markers of, 94
in Mastery Blueprint, 20–21
paradigm shifts and, 67, 69
paradox of, 98–101

redefined, 92
survival mode, 103, 104, 149
sustainability, 107, 141–142
SWOT analysis, 206

T

trauma, 63–64
tuition costs, 23
21st Century Preparation, 193–209

U

uncertainty, 6, 8, 9, 48, 52, 57–58, 63–64. *See also* VUCA (volatility, uncertainty, complexity, ambiguity)

V

verbal communication, 122
vision, 104, 126
volatility, 57–58. *See also* VUCA (volatility, uncertainty, complexity, ambiguity)
VUCA (volatility, uncertainty, complexity, ambiguity), 57–58, 72, 143, 145

W

wages, 26, 43
wants, needs *vs.*, 102
Warlick, David, 189

wealth, 199–201
well-being
emotional, 61–62
health and, 146–158
loneliness and, 60
state of emotional, 61–62
state of financial, 52
stress and, 62–63
uncertainty and, 6
wholeness, 176
Whyte, William, 19
work disruption, 58–59
World War II, 17–18
written communication, 122

Y

Young, Margaret, 89